Testimonials

"I started reading it and couldn't put it down. Rod's stories are so interesting. Each chapter makes you think about applying the lesson to your own life."

Sue Burnett, *CEO Burnett Specialists*

"*Week Minded* feels deeply personal from the first page. You can tell it was written by someone who has lived a full professional life and never lost sight of what matters most. He writes the way he leads—thoughtfully, honestly, and with real care for the people involved. What stands out about *Week Minded* is how genuine it is. Rod isn't preaching or positioning himself as an authority. He's sharing lessons the same way he would in a conversation—openly, with humility, and without ego. *Week Minded* is a reminder that strong leadership starts with kindness, listening, and doing the right thing even when it's hard. Rod's stories reinforce that you can be thoughtful and principled, practical and human, all at the same time. I'd recommend this book to anyone who values authentic leadership and believes that how you treat people really does matter."

Hang Bower, *Founder/CFO Ethos Consulting LC*

"It's a direct, no-nonsense 52-week guide for people who want results. Each week delivers one clear principle you can actually apply - to how you lead, how you work, how you make decisions, and how you run your life. It's practical thinking, uncomfortable truths, and steady pressure in the right direction. What makes this guide powerful is its discipline. One week at a time for reflection and action. It doesn't try to change you overnight; it builds consistency, judgment, and resilience over a year. The lessons compound. It's a refreshing way to approach growth and change."

Janette Marx, *CEO, Employbridge*

"Rod Branch has crafted a rare book that feels like messages from a mentor who has lived a life rich with stories, family, and friends. It shows us that our passions and 'red threads' shape us in ways we often only recognize later. This is Rod's voice at its truest: encouraging, grounded, and full of love for the reader."

Juliet Breeze, *MD, CEO, Next Level Medical*

"Rod brings an incredible amount of depth with the vast and vivid depictions of stories that bring further relevance to his journey. I so enjoyed reading the myriad of anecdotes that show an individual who has a passion for learning and knowledge woven into the fabric of the story. Rod's book is a must-read for anyone interested in the art of leadership & continuous learning. Rod has a great knack for storytelling that kept me on the edge of my seat for the entire book. I wholeheartedly endorse this wonderful depiction of a life well-lived."

Alan Brush, *Partner, Solution Spark*

"Rod Branch has crafted a masterclass in transformative insight, wrapped in a warm embrace - like curling into a warm blanket on a crisp day. The perfect blend of self-care and rest for the nervous system: soothing, grounding, and deeply human."

Sarah Kouba, *GM, Lone Star Groundwater Conservation District*

"Rod's stories and life lessons feel like sitting down with a trusted friend over a warm cup of coffee and a conversation that stays with you long after it ends. *Week-Minded* will strengthen your spirit. This isn't simply a collection of stories and wisdom — it is a guide to living with transparency, authenticity, and genuine care for others."

Liz Townsend, *Senior Partner, Allen Austin Consulting*

"People sometimes brag about 'graduating from the school of hard knocks' like it's a badge of honor to fumble through life. I'm thankful when people like Rod go out and do difficult things, learn hard lessons, gather and curate a lifetime of those lessons, and then present them on a platter for all of us to gain wisdom so we don't endure the same struggles."

Julian Pugh, *Division Operations Manager*

"I enjoy the honesty, vulnerability and relatability of your stories. I would use this as a nightly chapter read to turn my brain off from electronics and work, and read something *real* to unwind and feel the humanity of it."

Heidi Peters, *Sales Manager*

Week Minded

52 Reflections on Leading and Living

One Week, One Story, One Measure at a Time

Week Minded

52 Reflections on Leading and Living

One Week, One Story, One Measure at a Time

ROD BRANCH

BranchWater
Press

BranchWater
Press

BranchWater Press books may be purchased for educational, business or sales promotional use. For information please write: rod@BranchWaterPress.com or visit: branchwaterpress.com.

Production and creative provided by Epiphany Creative Services
Photographs on the back cover and pages 6, 86, and 136 by Whitney Hamilton Photography. Used with permission.
Printed in the United States of America
Library of Congress Cataloging-in-Publication Data
Library of Congress Control Number: 2026902683

FIRST EDITION
AUTHOR - 1st ed.
TITLE: Week Minded: 52 Reflections on Leading and Living, One Week, One Story, One Measure at a Time
p. cm.

ISBN: Paperback: 979-8-9942932-9-4
ISBN: Hardcover: 979-8-9942932-2-5
ISBN: eBook: 979-8-9942932-5-6

1. BUS041000 BUSINESS & ECONOMICS / Management
2. SEL021000 SELF-HELP / Motivational & Inspirational

Distributed by Ingramspark
26 10 9 8 7 6 5 4 3 2 1

Dedication

To my wife, Reneé, my family and friends who are still teaching me to be a complete human being, thank you. You've shown me that caring isn't a weakness and that learning never ends.

We're all trying to figure it out,
one week, one story, one act of kindness at a time.

We're on this road together, and that matters more than anything.

Table of Contents

Foreword

By Dr. Taryn Marie Stejskal

#1 *Wall Street Journal* bestselling author of *The 5 Practices of Highly Resilient People* and Founder and Chief Resilience Officer of The Resilience Leadership Institute (RLI)

Resilience is not built in theory.

It is built in lived moments—often ordinary, sometimes brutal, always formative.

That is why *Week Minded* matters.

When Rod Branch first asked me to write the foreword for this book, I smiled—and then promptly misspelled the word "foreword" in my correspondence with him. More than once. As someone who is dyslexic, I am no stranger to seeing the world differently or misspelling words. At first, I laughed it off. But the more I sat with Rod's words, the more fitting that mistake became. Because this foreword is not just a foreword to the pages that follow—it is an invitation to move *forward*. Thoughtfully. Intentionally. One week at a time.

Rod does not offer you platitudes, productivity hacks, or the illusion that leadership—or life—can be mastered through willpower alone. What he offers instead is something far more enduring, something evermore precious; he offers you, the reader, perspective earned the hard way, wisdom distilled through experience, and an invitation to reflect—one week at a time—on who you are today and who you're becoming tomorrow.

As a person who earned their doctorate, invested two decades studying resilience, served as an executive in Fortune 50 companies, and completed fellowships funded by the National Institutes of Health (NIH) on neuropsychology, I have spent decades studying how humans adapt, endure, and grow through disruption. Across industries, cultures, and life stages, the data tells us this: people do not build resilience by avoiding hardship. They build resilience by courageously facing the inevitable challenges, changes, and complexities of life, then making meaning from these experiences and integrating their knowledge and life lessons into a revised identity, rather than allowing difficulty to fracture them. This is the body of work that culminated in *The Five Practices of Highly Resilient People: Why Some Flourish When Others Fold*, which became a #1 *Wall Street Journal* bestseller. But even with all that research, I will tell you this plainly: resilience is learned most deeply through lived experience. And lived experience is exactly what Rod brings to these pages.

Week Minded is not a book you race through. It is a book you return to. A book you savor. You can open it to a single week that speaks to you—a lesson that meets you in a season of clarity, struggle, or change—and let that chapter serve as its own guide for that moment in time. Or you can read it cover to cover, allowing the reflections to build on one another, trusting the arc that slowly emerges. Both approaches are intentional. Life rarely unfolds in straight lines, and this book honors that truth.

Week Minded's power lies not in grand declarations, but in honest truths—stories that linger because they feel familiar. You will recognize yourself in these moments: standing at an unexpected crossroads, navigating responsibility and loss, and discovering that leadership is less about authority and more about presence, care, and courage.

What struck me most as I read was how deeply this book understands a principle I teach often: resilience lives at the intersection of awareness, connection, and choice.

Rod begins with awareness—becoming the student of your own life. Before we can lead others well, we must appraise ourselves honestly. We get to look within and make friends with the person we are today.

Not the curated external version. The real one. The authentic and vulnerable one. The one that is flawed and imperfect and still learning.

From there, Rod explores resilience not as grit-for-grit's-sake, but as adaptive strength—the kind forged in uncertainty, reinvention, responsibility, and loss. Resilience reveals itself in the narrow gates of adversity. You do not exit those gates unchanged. As I often say, you do not bounce back. You bounce *forward*, emerging more evolved—wiser, more grounded, more human.

Finally, Rod brings us home to connection. Because no amount of competence can replace caring. No title outperforms trust. No legacy exists without relationship. Leadership, at its core, is relational wisdom in action. These are time-honored truths, and yet, in an age of AI and technologificaton of our lives, Rod's insights remind us that what matters most, the humanity within all of us, can and will never be replaced with AI.

Throughout these reflections, you will notice something increasingly rare: humility. Rod does not write as someone who has it all figured out. He writes as someone still paying attention. Still learning. Still willing to say, *Here's what happened. Here's what it taught me. Maybe it will help you too.*

That posture matters.

In my work, I often remind leaders that resilience is not about having all the answers or being unbreakable. It is about being bendable without breaking, strong without becoming hardened, capable without becoming disconnected. This book models that beautifully. It shows us that caring is not weakness—it is capacity. That optimism is not denial—it is discipline. And that legacy is not what we leave behind—it is how we show up for others, consistently, over time.

If you are reading this book during a season where you are seeking deeper clarity amidst confusion, let it deepen your wisdom.

If you are reading it during a season of struggle, let it steady you.

If you are reading it while standing at the edge of change, let it remind you that you are not alone.

We are living in a time when resilience is needed more than ever—not just to show up in our daily lives, but to give us the courage and capacity to forge the chaos and uncertainty that defines so much of the world today. This book does not promise easy answers. What it offers is something better: a steady companion, a reflective pause, and a reminder that growth often begins with intention.

One week.

One reflection.

One choice at a time.

That is how resilient lives are built.

I am honored to write the foreword for a book that invites us all to move forward by way of harnessing our resilience, to courageously face challenge in service of knowing that expanded clarity, wisdom, confidence, and compassion await us on the other side.

Let's begin.

Introduction

Week Minded is your motivational slingshot to start every week. Every new week deserves a fresh start, a spark of purpose, and a reminder that growth begins with intention. Whether you're a busy mom or dad trying to determine how to attend to every tug of your apron strings, a busy midcareer professional navigating conflicting priorities, or someone at a career intersection wondering what you should be thinking about most, this book is for you—with love.

Maybe you're skimming these pages on a lunch break. Maybe you're stranded in an airport at seven a.m. with a cold beer and a little time to think. What matters most is that you showed up—open to learning from a life stitched together by hard knocks, good luck, and the grace of others who helped me sidestep bigger mistakes.

I didn't write this book to hand you a blueprint, a checklist, or some magic infographic for success. Life doesn't work that way. Each of us is shaped by our own mix of genes, circumstances, and choices, or, as Dr. Taryn Marie says, "challenges, changes, and complexities."[1] What I can offer is a window into some true stories—my failures and second chances, unexpected acts of bravery, and moments of faith, optimism, and generosity that showed up often unearned. What I've learned after nearly seven decades is this: Grace and humility carry more weight than pride and perfection ever will.

Music is a recurring theme in this book, and the anchoring thought that has played first chair in my family's life is a horn that I cannot play.

It belonged to my dad. This horn, a cornet in particular—much like a trumpet—is an example of my dad's pursuit of something he loved and his desire to play an instrument in both a marching band and a stage band. And he was good at it. It was his "red thread," which is the intersection of what you love and what you are good at.

Marcus Buckingham brought this ancient idea of the red thread back to life in his book *Love + Work: How to Find What You Love, Love What You Do, and Do It for the Rest of Your Life.*[2] East Asian cultures had the idea that fate is an invisible red thread connecting individuals, thoughts, and processes, much like the "scarlet thread" representing blood and referred to by the ancient Hebrews. If you can discover those red threads soon enough in your personal history and you can lean into them, even if they have little to do with your current profession, someday they will "play" a part in your success.

By the way, success is simply gleaning satisfaction from an effort. For me, for my dad, and for much of my immediate family, I can point to red threads connected to music, dance, public speaking, culinary arts, medical treatment, and deep caring that no one saw being a huge difference-maker in our lives. But they were. My hope for you is that in these many stories you can discover your own red threads. I hope that you draw courage, peace, motivation, and inspiration, propelling you toward the challenges life will hurl at you each week.

The book is divided into four sections to provide a logical flow of ideas. The first is more self-reflective, awakening an awareness of yourself. The next is about how challenges create the resilience and that resilience is necessary to do hard things. Then we explore the wisdom of leveraging crucial relationships for learning and maturity. We then slide to the end with leaving a legacy and what legacy truly means. What will people say when you leave the room or when you leave this world?

Maya Angelou often reminded us that people may forget the words we say to them but never the feeling we gave them. I am a social scientist. I read research papers. I enjoy data-mining. For a long time I was convinced that data and research were the way to learn and to convince someone else of a concept. However, there is an abundance of research showing that, in learning, we retain more when the "data" and lessons are relatable in stories and in how those lessons make us feel. For years, I dismissed storytelling as unscientific dreaming. I was wrong. Stories are how learning sticks. We remember most what we feel whether the life lesson comes from a fable or a true story. Stories are how we pass wisdom forward, not so much in the proof of data and science.

If taken to heart, these stories will widen your sense of what's possible in leading and living. As my friend Wendell says, "It all adds up." We are the sum of our experiences, and we are deeply influenced by the five people with whom we spend the most time.

So here is your first life lesson in this book: Take care of yourself and care intently. Do something grounding each week, even if it's just five minutes—like reading and reflecting on one chapter in this book. You'll meet your people, your work, and your chaos with more clarity if you begin from a place of peace and resolve. Caring is not fluff. It is the anchor value. Caring is the beginning of the red thread tying together every meaningful virtue—love, humility, forgiveness, generosity, and community. They're all neighbors on the same cul-de-sac. Lead with caring, toward yourself and others, and your decisions, relationships, and results will follow.

As you sit with these stories, laugh, cry a little, breathe, and reflect. Remember, you are enough and you are not alone. Take comfort. Many have walked in similar shoes. Celebrate your wins. Forgive your stumbles, but keep an inventory of your lessons. Acknowledge the people who brighten your world, and tell them often how they make you feel. Forgive those who failed you. Make this your weekly ritual. And if this book was a gift, thank the person who gave it to you—even if that person was you. I care about you as a fellow human being just trying to figure out this thing called life. Let's find your red thread—one week, one story, one act of kindness at a time. Let's begin.

"Let yourself be silently drawn by the strange pull of what you really love. It will not lead you astray."

—Rumi

Part I – Awakening Awareness

Becoming the Student of Your Own Life

Everyone's story begins with awareness—not of others but of self. Before we can inspire, we must first awaken. Awakening awareness is the introspective process of garnering the courage to step into uncertain spaces, to reflect on our own beliefs, and to challenge the comfortable boundaries that keep us from growing.

These first weeks invite you to take inventory of the life you've been living and the leader you're becoming—intentionally or not. They call you to journal, to reflect, to question what "success" really means, and to rediscover the value of curiosity over judgment. Hopefully, in line with the book's recurring theme of musical talent and music appreciation, you will discover your own set of rhythms and the talents you are good at and love doing. You never know when they will show up in your life as huge advantages.

Here, leadership isn't a position; it's a presence. It begins when you stop striving to be known and start striving to be *worth* knowing. When you trade comfort for curiosity, you begin the lifelong practice of becoming the student of your own life.

Week 1

Discover your horn of plenty.

"What a Wonderful World"
—Louis Armstrong

Life Lesson

Near the end of his life my dad shared something quietly painful with me, something I think too many people carry without saying it out loud. He told me that he felt disappointed in how far he had gotten in his career. I was a bit shocked. He said he was disappointed, not because he didn't work hard; he did. Not because he didn't achieve; he did that too. Because he never made it "all the way to the top" of where he thought he deserved to be in corporate America, or the "global" corporate in his case. That broke my heart.

See, Dad spent most of his career honoring the advice of his father, who told him, "You've got to learn the business from the ground up!" He spent many years working as a field engineer, away from the corporate office, braving the elements and troubleshooting real engineering problems in the moment. He traveled most of his life domestically and then spent the last years living abroad, doing the same field engineering, only with people from diverse cultures, often through interpreters. It was some of the hardest work in the oil field.

He looked at his colleagues who had reached the boardroom, who worked in the shiny glass towers at corporate headquarters their entire career, on display for the execs who would guide their advancement, and he felt like he had come up short. He compared their polished résumés and corner offices to his own long days in field offices, negotiating with unenlightened foreign executives in the dustiest corners of the planet, in the harshest conditions.

Beyond that, being raised in the South and mostly central Louisiana, there was a bit of bred racism, a bit of "they don't look like me" mentality instilled—something that had to be overcome to be productive in this world. It isn't the kind of cultural training that prepares you for an international career. There was racial brainwashing even as a child before it had a name. Plus, he was earning his work stripes in the mid-1960s when the race war was ON! Now, in the 1980s and 90s, he was faced with getting these "foreigners" to want to do the work the oil company needed them to do. They were employed by the company under an agreement that a certain number of locals had to work for the joint venture. Dad struggled a bit in Canada—his first international assignment—seeing some of the workers as lazy, in his opinion. He overcame that. Then he had to engage Bedouins in the Saharan desert. Learning some of the language helped, and his driver, Ahmed, whom he had for safety reasons, was Muslim and helped Dad understand how Dad was different and what attitudes and behaviors were needed to navigate the locals in Cairo more effectively.

The reindeer herders above the Russian Arctic Circle were the biggest challenge yet. He found himself in fabric teepee homes, not even a yurt, in whiteout conditions, eating raw reindeer meat dipped in blood to show his acceptance of the indigenous, and he hoped the same for them accepting him. Yes, he did it. He ate the meat. The Russian oil field operations that existed before the Americans arrived were very dangerous. There were few rules regarding safety. People were injured or killed as a matter of routine. Dad kept them safe, aided the community by supporting Russian orphanages, and ate meals with people who were not like him. He saw them, and he made sure they felt seen. He earned these people's trust doing things in places most of us can't find on a map. These are Mother Theresa and Medal of Freedom level moments—that no one in the shiny glass tower ever saw.

It's easy, too easy, to fall into the trap of measuring ourselves by someone else's scoreboard. To chase titles, cars, curated lives, and social media highlight reels, comparing our confident truth to someone else's filtered fiction. In that comparison, we forget to celebrate the climb. I've done it too. I once thought I'd be a lawyer—the attorney job I thought I needed to be "seen" as important. I had the brains, the motivation, and the ambition. Life, or the "world" and its random acts, had other plans. Instead, I got a hard-won bachelor's degree in a field I never wanted and traveled across the country in an un-air-conditioned, hand-me-down 1965 Chevy, living at times in rented mobile homes and getting to know the locals in all the towns where my Chevy broke down. It wasn't glamorous. It wasn't easy. It shaped me. It gave me the grit, the compassion, and yes, the heartbreak, that now forms the soul of this book you're holding.

There is an essential part of this story I must add here. When my grandfather was struggling in 1948—well, one of the many times he was struggling—he drove a milk truck delivering milk in DeRidder, Louisiana. He "hired" my dad as a young lad for one dollar per day to run the milk from the truck to the front porches and to bring the empty milk bottles back to the truck. My dad saved all of his dollars he made doing that work for my grandfather. He used that money to buy a cornet, similar to a trumpet, to satisfy his long-held desire to play an instrument. He learned to play the cornet in the high school marching band and played in the stage band after football games for the sock hops. Sock hops were school dances in the 1950s that took place in the gym where street shoes were not allowed on the polished floors. So most people danced in socks—thus, "sock" hops. Dad was doing double duty because he was a star running back for the high school football team, so he had to play, shower, and then run to the gym to play in the stage band. He played football and played in the band because each filled a gap for him. He was good at both, and he loved both. So, on with the story.

It was unfathomable to me that my dad could not fully appreciate what he accomplished in his career, let alone the bravery of my poor mom, being dragged through the world's mudholes. So I did what I do in my job and what I am starting to do with this book: I sat him down with kindness and asked him to zoom out. To take a wider look. "You were born on a sharecropper's farm," I said, then continued,

> "You picked cotton in the tortuous Louisiana sun. You had an eighth grader's dream to be a professional engineer with no reasonable path to affording college. No mentors—few in your extended family had even graduated from high school. One hot and humid Louisiana afternoon August 1952, you loaded the car you borrowed, armed with only a dream and some hope that you would find a way to go to college to be an engineer and headed out for McNeese College in Lake Charles, Louisiana. You tried out for the college football team and at the end of the day, the coach put his arm around your neck and told you about making the team as a running back. Then he told you he

> had no scholarship for you, and because the coach told you he didn't have a scholarship for you, you said, "Then I can't play." Then you went to the car and dug out your horn, still in the velvet-lined wooden case it came in. You went down the hall to the band room and asked to try out for the band. You made the band, and that horn got you a band scholarship to college. That horn changed the entire trajectory of our family's life."

I went on,

> "You got a master's degree in petroleum engineering. You built an international career. You raised three kids who earned a total of five college degrees, and you kept us grounded, even while the work moved you all over the world. You once sold all your company stock to pay your parents' medical bills. You stayed humble. You made it further than anyone would've ever guessed you could. Dad, it's not about how far you got. It's about how far you came. You leaned in hard on what you loved - football and music. And you were good at both, but there is no way you could have known that that horn would change the course of your life and all of our family's lives."

> *"Success is to be measured not so much by the position that one has reached in life as by the obstacles which he has overcome while trying to succeed."*[5]
>
> —Booker T. Washington

If I, myself, had taken a different path, it might have gone badly and I would have been an oil field pumper, or it might have gone according to plan and I would have been an Oklahoma City attorney—never leaving Oklahoma for the rest of my life. Either way, I wouldn't have had these stories. I wouldn't have met the mentors who rewired my thinking. I wouldn't have sought out the wisdom of the great minds in people and leadership. I wouldn't be me. I kind of like this version of me. I've learned to forgive myself for screwing up the law career thing.

There are several lessons here. I still see it in action in my life today.

1. Volunteer to lean in and do the things that you love and that you are good at. Those are your red threads, as Marcus Buckingham describes in Love + Work. Somehow, someday they will serve you. That horn went from an enjoyable pastime to the Sherpa, the treasure map, and the guiding light that got my dad his engineering degree.
2. Take stock of how far you've come. Celebrate the ride, or as the enlightened new generation call it, "the journey." Savor it. Let it anchor you. However, don't get too comfortable. This isn't a license to settle or a free pass to coast. *Aspire. Keep climbing. Keep growing.* My dad kept the faith, as linear as he was, navigating life more with a slide rule than with his emotional desires, and I loved that about him.

What I hope for you is this: When you reach the end of your road, you won't measure your life by your final rank or salary. I hope you measure it by how many of your joys you pursued and how much of your heart you gave, how many people you helped, how many obstacles you hurdled when nobody thought you could. What was your horn of plenty? Who were your Bedouins? Who were your reindeer herders? Who were the Canadian field workers you had to win over?

Nearing the end of your life—oh, and we rarely know when that is—I hope you raise your glass in celebration. I hope you can see how far you've come and smile. I hope you have squeezed out every last drop of pride you deserve to feel, no matter how far you've come. It's your journey—no one else's.

In the forty-three days between my mom's and my dad's deaths in 2022, my dad and I talked every day. One day, unsolicited, he said, "You know, son. I've been thinking about what you said. That thing about how far you've come. When we moved from Louisiana to Oklahoma, following the oil field dance card circuit, my dad couldn't find Oklahoma on a map. We might as well have moved to the moon. He never understood what I did for a living, and that hurt me a little. He couldn't appreciate what it took to do what I did. I now see what you mean. I came a long way."

As he looked out the window to the fall wind deleafing the oaks in the front of the house, not knowing he was weeks from the end of his time, maybe his head turn was to hide the little tear that began to form. He went on, "It is inconceivable that I even got out of DeRidder, Louisiana, much less ran a joint venture in the Russian Arctic." I think he said, "Thank you," to me somewhere in those words. I think he was turning the corner at the top of a tall emotional hill, where he could finally look back down the road to see how far he had come and to know, maybe for the first time, the elevation he had achieved. And based on the way I brokered our exchange, I think he could see the value in what I do for a living too—maybe our hearts grew two sizes together that day.

I couldn't have asked for a better final thought.

Week 2

Step into the space.

"Into the Great Wide Open"

—Tom Petty

Life Lesson

I usually start this story with the fact that it is a three-beer conversation, and I am willing to have anyone else buy. Therefore, this week's message is a bit longer than the rest.

It was 1986. We were 1,200 miles south of the North Pole and 250 miles above the Arctic Circle. I was a drilling engineer in the oil fields of the Alaskan Arctic, worlds away from anything I thought I would ever see. There were Arctic foxes, musk oxen, caribou, and polar bears in the wild, and the Northern Lights appeared from time to time to light up the sky in strange technicolor. I was transferred there because the work in the "Lower 48" had dried up with the latest oil bust. If you don't know, the oil and gas business is an eight-second ride (that's rodeo lingo for "hang on as long as you can before you get bucked off"). If you know, you know.

We would catch a chartered plane on Monday of the hitch week and fly two hours from Anchorage to Deadhorse, Alaska (you can't make this stuff up), where the Prudhoe Bay oil field sits between the Brooks Range mountains and the Arctic Ocean. The slope in elevation between the mountains and the ocean is nicknamed "The Slope" or "The North Slope." The charter jet was configured where half the plane was for cargo and half was for passengers. Once we arrived over Deadhorse, the pilots would make one pass over the airfield to ensure there were no caribou on the runway. When parked on the ground, we were greeted by a Bluebird school bus, the preferred transportation in Deadhorse, and were shuttled to the base camp. At base camp, we shared a room with one other field worker and took the still-warm bunk of a person ending their shift that day.

All the housing, office buildings, and production units on the Slope were manufactured elsewhere, and some required shipping through the Panama Canal. As such, the width of some modules was determined by the width of the locks along the canal. When the ice receded from the Arctic coast, the modules were shipped on barges and pulled by tractors into place on risers.

I arrived for my first "hitch" in February 1986. We worked twelve-hour shifts each day, seven straight days, then reversed the process to return home to Anchorage a week later. It was dark almost all the time during the winter with the sun making a big smudge on the horizon in the middle of the "day"—whenever "daytime" was; it was hard to tell.

One day, the wind chill was ninety-five degrees below zero and black-dark. We were well dressed in $1,200 (in 1986 dollars) worth of cold-weather gear. There were boots, gloves, socks, and an outfit that started with a down shirt, then down overalls over that, and a down, coyote-fur-ringed hooded parka on top of that. There would be many days like that one when a "flesh-freeze warning" was issued. We might as well have been on the moon.

What happened to my life? Where was I? The oil and gas business had been on a downward slide, and the price of oil was inching toward the unthinkable, shutting down even the Alaskan oil production. Fun fact: when you drill wells in the Arctic, the ground is frozen the first two thousand feet down—that's two-fifths of a mile. If you shut a well in (i.e., turn it off), the warm flow of oil and gas from deeper in the earth will stop and the well will freeze, so an unprecedented decision to shut down might be extremely expensive. Getting wells thawed to return to production is very risky. We never took the risk of shutting down wells in the field. We just kept it flowing so the warm flow of oil kept things thawed.

I had decided almost five years before the transfer to Alaska that I had made a career mistake becoming an engineer. It didn't suit me, and this little trip to see Santa did not change my mind. I thought I was stuck being an engineer for the rest of my life like my dad. I didn't know that people changed careers—ever. I didn't know you could go from "engineer" to anything else. I hated my work life, and I figured that if you are doing production and drilling engineering in the Arctic and you still are not curious and challenged by it, you are for sure in the wrong career.

The impact of working on the Slope on the family was also grueling. My youngest son was six months old when we moved, and he always changed a great deal each week I was gone—beginning to talk, crawl, and walk were big moments that were missed while I was away. I intellectually knew it was seven on and seven off, but it always felt more like eleven on and three off. I missed my family.

A few months in, I was in a staff meeting at base camp with about fifteen operations and engineering types and the president of Sohio Alaska Production Company, which became BP Alaska. He asked the assembly of engineers and operations if anyone had public speaking experience. No one raised a hand. After an awkward silence, I half-raised my hand to explain that I had spoken on college campuses to engineering recruits a few times. "Branch, you're it!" he said, motioning me to follow him to another office.

Behind a closed door, he told me about a very strange assignment. I was going to get on one of our Bluebird school buses on a microphone and explain to "some people" how we could develop oil reserves anywhere in the Arctic without damaging the environment. Confidently, I said I could do that. In the 1980s, there wasn't a lot of "asking" people to do things or checking in on our mental health—whether you were stressed about the windchill of ninety-five degrees below zero or had separation anxiety about your kids and dog. You kept that "weakness" to yourself. You did what you were told and didn't complain—there were few questions accepted. The feeling was that if you showed any sign that you didn't want this job, there were ten others with bags packed at the airport ready to take it. I had only one question: "Who are these people I would be speaking to on the bus?" He rocked back in his chair and said very matter-of-factly, "The United States Senate Energy Committee and the Secretary of Interior."

I'm not sure that I remember verbatim what was said in the next few minutes. I was still processing what I thought I heard. I swallowed hard. I was twenty-eight years old. In what universe does this happen? But here was my chance to do something as close to my elusive attorney career as I would ever get. My intuition was that I would be good at it, because I knew I would love doing it. Public speaking was easy for me, a skill that would serve me well in successive careers.

So, I did it. I greeted them after learning the correct way to address the congressional detail as "Senator" and "Mr. Secretary." We made a stop at "Mile Post Zero," the beginning of the Trans Alaska Pipeline System (TAPS), a four-foot-diameter, earthquake-resistant pipe that moved the Alaskan crude oil from the Slope to the Port of Valdez near Anchorage. After the bus trip, I was invited to fly with the group in a Sikorski helicopter to the undeveloped Arctic National Wildlife Refuge (ANWR) next door to witness a natural oil seep where oil was bubbling up out of the ground like in Jed Clampett's backyard. This wasn't "pollution"; this was nature's doing. It was so cool.

There was plenty of time along the way to live vicariously as an elected official with long conversations with the senators. I was interested in how they found their legislative assistants, how much time they spent in their home states, and whether they moved their families to Washington or not. I became friends with Senator Barbara Mikulski and Senator Don Nickles that day in ANWR.

After that day, we had formal internal debriefs on what we learned and strategized about how to further our cause of getting ANWR opened for oil and gas exploration and development while protecting the interests of the locals who had been living there for centuries. We worked hard to take care of the Indigenous people. We helped them drag whales onto the land. We supplied them with snow machines (snowmobiles) and other equipment, not to appease them for the inconvenience of the oil and gas operations but to show them what progress can do for them while ensuring that we did not damage the land they held so sacredly. We were "in" with the locals, but the onlooking press and special interest groups were intent on telling the world a different story, showing our operations in a negative light. We were depicted as ruthless money grabbers and careless polluters of the pristine coastline. We tried to show the other side of it, showing footage of the good we did—footage that never made the news or headlines. That became my resolve, to tell the true story.

As I listened to the press and watched them report, I would ask myself, *How did they get to work that day? Where did they think the materials came from used in the hospital where their child was born?* And if they bragged about riding the electric train to their office, I would ask where they thought most electricity used by trains came from? Most of it comes from natural gas. Even if we wanted to stop using it today, we couldn't. Our clothes, tennis shoes, and a zillion other products come from it. As I thought about my experiences over those few days, it dawned on me that I liked what I was doing. I felt good about protecting the land, and I was rather good at reporting the facts and making them relevant to the audience.

After only one day of helping with government affairs, I started thinking about having to go back to the *boring* world of drilling engineering (see what I did there?). Perhaps I could do more in another setting. I was doing well and holding my own intellectually at this government affairs level; maybe there was a way to use my skills to create greater impact across a broader segment of people. My mind began to race and to be open to something much greater.

Government affairs as a function was a little outside my comfort zone, but it couldn't be stranger or more difficult than forty below zero on the frozen tundra trying to start a Tioga heater and risking freezing to death because no one knew where you were in the field. GPS was not a thing yet. Most of the training we got in the Arctic ended each sentence with, "And you could die!" That day, conducting that tour, it was like taking a ten-year-old boy to the circus, letting him see the lion tamer up close for one minute, and then closing the curtain on the tent and telling him the show was over for him.

Back into engineering I went.

About a week later, depressed, I was working on one of the production pads, daydreaming about my day working with the Washington, DC, folks. Drilling and production pads were gravel pads where the land was built up above grade. It was stable, compacted ground so that the heavy drilling rigs and other service company equipment would not sink when the ground thawed slightly in the spring. A pickup truck pulled up next to us. It was the president again. He got out and greeted us, sprinkling his hello with a few well-placed f-bombs. He pulled me aside for a conversation. He told me that I had done a (damn) good job of touring the dignitaries and that the feedback was that the government affairs team for BP wanted me to go to meetings with them in Washington. It would be a long-term assignment as an assistant to the lobbyists. The president sheepishly asked if I would be interested in that kind of work, but it would mean that, for the foreseeable future, I would not be working on the North Slope as an engineer. He was apologetic.

Now, this was startling news. I had only dabbled in lobbying for a day, but I had been unknowingly preparing for it my entire life. The uncertainty and impostor feelings set in briefly, but for once, I think I recognized a welcomed challenge and a fork in the road worth taking. I tried to hide my excitement. I thought to myself, Wow, what in the actual heck? In what universe? And then I said yes to working with the lobbyists.

So we were off. I took the red-eye every other Sunday night, leaving Anchorage at two a.m. and arriving in DC in early afternoon. I bought suits at the Alexander Julian store in Washington. My days were filled with "call-ups" on "The Hill." Call-ups are appointments with legislative assistants (LAs) and congresspeople inside the legislative office buildings that flank the Capitol building. The work was challenging physically and mentally. But it was the kind of challenge I enjoyed. The job required late nights out, entertaining the LAs and influencing them with knowledge, data, and three martinis. Then at six thirty the next morning, we had a debrief on what I had learned. This is a young person's game: always on, no sleep, lots of alcohol, and a full day's journey on each end of the week. As time went on, I met with the Undersecretary of Commerce and even got to have a meeting in the Gothic-looking, French Second Empire style circa 1871 Executive Office Building next to the White House. The doors looked like those at the gates of Oz. It is mostly offices for White House staff. I came to realize that this was my heaven.

As I look back, the happenstance of volunteering to speak to the college engineering groups and raising my hand, not even knowing it was for the Bluebird bus talk, opened a door and opened my mind to alternative careers. I no longer limited my future to engineering and what I knew at that moment. I could see further down the road now, beyond the staid role of a staff engineer. I was now receptive to what I could learn looking forward. I moved from locked-down engineer to "technocrat" lobbyist in a matter of seconds. And it was all in the bravery of a half-raised hand in a room in the frozen Arctic. A lesson here is to volunteer for activities outside your normal course of work if they interest you and you find yourself good at them. (Thank you, Marcus Buckingham, for the "red thread" idea.) Build those skills that may not be in your career path yet. They just might be the skills that change your life.

Step into the space.

Week 3

Find your place to reflect and be inspired.

"The Sound of Silence"

–Simon and Garfunkel

Life Lesson

The "Bourbon Room" in my home is my inspirational home base. It is the place of early morning writings, focus, and silent deep thoughts. My wife is a natural at decorating and would have loved to have this space as a tearoom or sitting room, so having given this small room to me was one of the kindest gestures she could have made. She also lets me know when my souvenir addiction makes the room feel crowded and claustrophobic.

The Bourbon Room is the home of what we call the Confab, a curated group of HR deep thinkers gathering for a libation, light bites, and unabridged sharing. This room—cozy, familiar, silently powerful—is a sanctuary of sorts. It is where I go to remember who I am.

When you spend your life with people at work who depend on you and people in your family who rely on you, there is this pressure. The things I enjoyed—books, journaling, and podcasts—were being crowded out by the noise of the world. Here, I could wall off the hustle and settle into the feelings of past victories, time with my dad, and the wonder of my kids' lives. I could get in touch with the jailed feelings of losing my parents so quickly and emote for the first time. It was safe there. No judgment. There is a photo from a family golf outing that brings me peace just by looking at it. A couple of my guitars hang nearby, one slightly out of tune, both full of songs that still live inside me. Art that says, "Music is what feelings sound like."

The Bourbon Room is truth!

Nearby sits a stack of napkins imprinted with a scene from the room and with the words "The Bourbon Room—Where we make only pour decisions." There are echoes of my Washington, DC, days and a small Russian accordion—homage to my dad's work in the Russian Arctic. On one shelf, a clay hand print from my baby grandson, Ashton Branch, and a photo of my daughter Jordan dressed in her 2004 Super Bowl NFL dance costume. An autographed set list from a Deana Carter show given to me by daughter Katie is propped behind my picture of Senator Don Nickles and me at Mile Post Zero. Then there is my newly acquired barrel top with the inscription denoting me as a "Tennessee Squire," a distinction from Jack Daniels distillery made possible by my nomination by bestselling author and fellow squire Gair Maxwell. Each Squire is afforded only one nomination of another Squire in his or her lifetime.

There are keepsakes from our thirtieth wedding anniversary at the Kentucky Derby and a blanket from Prison City Brewing in Lake Placid. None of them is expensive. All of them are priceless. I've been to and seen many inspiring places and scenes, but the Bourbon Room is my home base where my feelings are magically converted to prose. The stillness allows me to process the convictions I hold deep.

I've been inspired by the rhythmic plop of raindrops on downtown Bozeman streets, the snow on Breckenridge rooftops, and a hundred-year-old farmhouse in Saranac, New York, looking at a white church that held generations of stories across the river. And the simplicity of the early mornings at Barton Creek near Austin with deer meandering across the greens and a silence that somehow said everything I needed to hear. I've been inspired in Aberdeen, Scotland, at the Ferryhill House Hotel while I watched locals laugh over their pints. Also while looking out from my dock in our lake community in Cypress, Texas, where I occasionally entertain the neighbors with live music. I have a gas fire pit—perfect for a "wee dram," a fire, and a light sweater in the fall.

But the real work, the shaping and reshaping of ideas? That happens right here in the Bourbon Room. Funny how certain places become sacred because of what they awaken in us. Rumi said it best: "Let yourself be silently drawn by the strange pull of what you really love. It will not lead you astray." That strange pull? That's *inspiration*. It's emotional energy. It's the gentle power that helps you rise above what burdens you.

The Bourbon Room is truth! I can be honest with myself that in my quest to provide a life for these people who suffered through the missteps of my early days, I was not the dad, husband, and human being that I could have been at times. I see now what I needed to be for them. I hurt deeply about that. I think that is part of the reason we are given grandchildren. It is the translation of the missed opportunities of our youth and the ever-present misplaced regrets and a new longing to pay it back in Pawpaw love. This book came to me because the stories are real and are mine. They are the raw, honest, sometimes painful moments that shaped me. In all the wishes for do-overs and the hardening life lessons I have discovered, they weren't wasted; they were necessary. I find them in the deep reflection of the Bourbon Room.

I remember times when my family of origin didn't have much money, and my parents' picnics out of the back of a 1964 Chevy Impala station wagon were made to feel like five-star events. That was abundance. That was love. It is akin to the story of ordinary loaves and fishes that fed the thousands. There wasn't much there, but what was there fed our souls. My life is rich because it's been real. Relationships gave me boundaries, backstops, and second chances. I've been blessed with people who helped me carry burdens I knew I could never lift alone. I owe them more than they'll ever know.

Honor the places and people that remind you who you are, because life isn't measured by what happens to us. It is defined by how we're *inspired to respond*. And if you are lucky enough to know what inspires you, don't wait to lean into it. Let it shape you, guide you, and give you the emotional energy to keep going, especially when it's hard. More than anything else, live your life gratefully every day. I know I am ... now.

To feed what inspires you is to give breath to the belly fire inside. It lifts your spirit and reminds you why it all matters. It doesn't have to be grand. It can be a single photo, a faded memory, a worn-out guitar string, a familiar scent, or a melody that stirs your soul. For me, inspiration doesn't come from things I own themselves; it comes from life behind them. Those things remind me of the people I've lived alongside. So let me offer this: Find what inspires you. Feed it. Protect it. Let it feed you back.

Find your place to reflect and be inspired. Feed that wolf!

Week 4

Take the road less traveled.

"My Way"
—*Frank Sinatra*

Life Lesson

It was around 2003, and I was doing what fathers do best: building a future for my kids. My younger son, Keaton, had a brilliant SAT score. He could've gone to college anywhere. And having spent much of his life in Texas, he chose Texas A&M—a solid, respectable, choice. His first semester went fine. Everything about his college lifestyle looked normal from the outside. By the second semester and into the third, it began to go sideways.

He picked up the guitar when he was very young. His older brother played. I played. His maternal grandfather played, and his maternal great grandmother played. In high school he formed a band, Antinothing, and he was hooked. He's a smart guy, so no telling how little he studied in high school, but he had the SAT score to get to a legit college.

Turns out, he was falling in love with music and out of love with schoolwork about that time, playing live in Northgate, A&M's high-energy district packed with bars, stages, and the kind of adrenaline that no eight a.m. lecture could compete with. Eventually, the truth became clear: He wasn't going to class. He was gigging. Living for the stage. So I made the call I thought was necessary. "Pack up. You're coming home."

I tried to steer him back to the "right" path. I laid out the plan: education, then a job, then a life. But the more I pushed, the more he drifted toward something else, something I couldn't quite understand. So finally, like many parents, I had to let go and let God.

What I didn't admit out loud back then was that I was secretly tailing him around Houston on weekends, watching him light up rooms with bands like the Sunset Strippers, the Foo Fakers, and Life as Lions. While I knew he was good, seeing him on stage made me realize just how good.

And he was happy.

And somehow, through it all, he found steady work, first at Apple, then at Microsoft. He wasn't just playing music. He was building something. He helped bring creative energy into the retail space, connecting with his community, and earned his way into solid benefits, stock plans, and career growth. I started thinking, "Okay, this isn't what I pictured, but maybe it's going to work out." Then he called with news that stopped my heart. "Dad, the band wants to move to Los Angeles. And I want to go." To be clear, he wasn't asking permission. He was informing me.

Here we go again. "What will you *do* for work?" I asked, trying not to sound panicked. He said calmly, "I'm talking to some companies out there." In the meantime, Microsoft had an assistant manager opening at their *only* store in LA, in *Beverly Hills*. Despite a sea of local candidates, my son, musician, non-degree-holder, got the job. He proceeded to use his relocation allowance to move the entire band from Houston to Glendale, California, and filmed a music video about the journey. They played the House of Blues on Sunset, got on Spotify, and *never once* paid to play. It was magic. Until it wasn't. He lived the relatively poor musician life with all his band members living in one house in LA. That went as planned for a few years.

As life happens, the bassist got married and moved back to Houston. The other band members hit their thirties, and dreams gave way to adult decisions. The band broke up. Another fork in the road for Keaton. But then ... another door opened. Microsoft called Keaton, this time from *headquarters*. They wanted him to move to Seattle to do international training. He said yes. He moved to Seattle and for his first assignment: London. A month abroad, helping new employees get their footing while he lived like a king in a foreign land. From Northgate to Notting Hill, he was living large.

And then, as if the story wasn't remarkable enough, he met and married Dr. Kate, a doctor of occupational therapy in Seattle. Kate is an only child. Her mom and dad were only children too. There were no brothers, sisters, aunts, uncles, or cousins. When he brought her to Houston for the first Christmas with this band of crazies, we were afraid we would scare her off. Our Christmas consists of rented bus pub crawls, Lotteria, which we call Mexican Bingo, a late night with champagne ("Shamps" as known at Maison Branche du Lac), eggnog (lactose-free for Keaton), *Christmas Vacation* in the Theater Room, then a huge breakfast cooked outside on the outdoor kitchen griddle with an all-day marathon of each person opening one present at a time. Going from an only child and humming "Silent Night" in front of a crackling fire to a backslapping, yuletide, icicle-slinging, nog-slurping, rocking around the Christmas tree, Cousin Eddy "Shitter's full," rowdy hangover-riddled holiday was a bit of a culture shift. She survived just fine. The COVID wedding was a brilliant white affair in a glassed-in atrium on the roof of an old hotel in Ballard, Washington. It was officiated by our family friend and my number one trivia partner, Olya! I was a proud papa. And Kate became daughter number three. Today, they live outside Seattle, raising our only Branch heir, in a home they own—*him*, a man working at one of the world's largest tech companies, and *her*, "Dr. Kate," enough said.

At their rehearsal dinner, I read part of Robert Frost's poem "The Road Not Taken": "Two roads diverged in a wood, and I, I took the one less traveled by, and that has made all the difference." Keaton took the road I didn't recognize, couldn't predict, and wouldn't have chosen for him. But that road took him somewhere extraordinary. And it taught me something I didn't see coming either: Sometimes the best thing a father can do is get out of the way and cheer from the sidelines. Because the view from the stands is amazing—watching your kid win *his* game, *his* way? Sometimes you have to let go and let the road less traveled be the way.

Week 5

No one should ever say,
"That's not my job.".

"We Can Work It Out"
—The Beatles

Life Lesson

Mom died on October 13 (not a Friday), 2022, of natural causes.

Knowing my dad would be alone with his thoughts, I spent almost every evening with him after Mom died. They had been married sixty-six years, and at eighty-eight years old, my dad was at a loss.

Dad and I were good friends. We loved golf, oil field stories, and Astros baseball. So many of my friends had already lost their dads, and *my* dad filled that gap for some of them. He was not only welcomed but sought after to join my buddies' escapades. Before my mom died, my friend Steve got Dad on Bluejack, Tiger Woods's course, north of Houston, and Steve, George, and I surprised my dad with a trip to play Pebble Beach. My sister had agreed to fly down and take care of my mom to allow him to do it. It would be the last golf trip he would make.

After Mom died and leading up to Thanksgiving, Dad decided he was going to get back in shape. He would test his ideas with me. He walked two miles without much trouble that day. That night I went to his house. He was proud of his walk and was encouraged that maybe getting back in shape enough to play golf again was a reasonable goal. He told me he planned to walk every other day to build his strength. I encouraged it and was excited for him, but the next day, he walked again—a day earlier than he'd committed to.

I was at work, and I got a call from my dad's phone. It was an EMT saying that my dad had fallen in the street. A neighbor my dad did not know had sat in the street with him until the ambulance showed up. The EMT said they were on their way to the emergency room. At a well-known hospital in Cypress, Texas, there was a very unfortunate series of mistakes. I am going to recount the absolute truth.

I met them at the hospital. He had fallen in the street while walking within sight of his house. He had a bleeding lip and a broken tooth and was complaining of pain in his side. When I got to the hospital, they had taken X-rays and said he was fine. Nothing was broken. He hobbled onto a wheelchair, and I loaded him into the SUV for the ride home. I took him back home with pain pills, and my wife, Reneé, an RN trained in wound care, met me at his house to treat and redress his wounds—much better than the MASH-unit job the ER nurses had done. By the morning, he could barely move. We continued with the pain regimen, and he was not getting better. I took him back to the hospital, and on the second exam, they found broken ribs. How can you miss that the first time in an ER? Isn't that what they do for a living?

They gave him more pain medicine with no other instructions about bowel issues with pain meds and said he could go home again. I could barely manage him. I was struggling getting him to his feet, and he could not move his bowels. It had been days. My sister came down early for Thanksgiving week to give me a break. She is the head of radiation therapy at a hospital in Oklahoma. Quickly she decided our dad needed to go back to the hospital. This time they admitted him.

My sisters and I were at the hospital Thanksgiving Day. The hospital had a free dinner in the cafeteria for families. While we were sitting there, the hospital CEO came through with his COO. They greeted everyone and said, "Let us know if we can do anything for your family while you are here."

Complications mounted, mostly related to Dad's bowels and pain killers. In a desperate move, a colonoscopy was done to move his bowel blockage. They tore his colon in a botched late-night emergency procedure with a skeleton staff on the holiday. He would need another surgery and now had a risk of sepsis, and a colostomy bag was in his future. Oh, and he coded on the table during the colonoscopy. He survived. The thing is, the doctor failed to tell us anything about him coding. The next morning on Black Friday, I was standing in his room with my middle-child sister. I noticed his blood pressure was beginning to fall rapidly, and his heart rate was slowing. Alarms started going off. No one was coming to check on him.

I went to the nurses' station right outside the room and said to the one young woman who could barely hear me over the alarms going off, "My dad seems to be coding, and no one is coming to check on him!" Her response as a medical professional and as a human being will be forever burned into my memory, as she said, "He's not my patient!" I leaned in and responded a bit firmer and still professionally, "I don't care if he's not your patient. Someone needs to see to him!" She held up her hand like a traffic cop, palm out and fingers extended like a starfish, and said, "Don't talk to me that way!" She got up from her comfortable chair and went *slowly* the opposite way down the hall away from his room. I was getting angry and decided the best thing would be for me to get out of the way and trust that they knew what they were doing. I retreated to the waiting area. I heard a commotion down the hall. Lots of yelling. My sister was wailing as they walked her toward me. I could see they were doing CPR on him. He had a DNR. I had to be the one to tell them to stop the compressions since by then they had broken all of the rest of his ribs. On November 25, 2022, Black Friday. I became an orphan.

So, let's see, they failed on finding the broken ribs, sent him home too soon, failed to manage the bowel lock, botched the colonoscopy, never told us they punctured his colon, he coded, never told us he coded, and he coded again that morning, and they failed to respond to the code. They accepted no responsibility for any of it. He was gone. The hospital later stated that everything they did for my dad was according to procedure and hospital protocol. Mr. CEO of this unnamed hospital, here's something you can do for us ... (comments are truncated as I relive that morning).

I suppose everyone looks for someone to blame in these inexplicable situations. There were so many mistakes. Maybe this was the "B" team working during the Thanksgiving holiday. We will never know the truth. As an engineer, my dad chose "Pi = 3.141592 ..." for his tombstone—fitting and precise. It's irrational, like the situation in the hospital where he died.

For a guy who always accepted responsibility and who always made others look good by helping them with their jobs, he was a victim of many who did none of that.

In a crisis where others are pleading for help, no one should ever say, "That's not my job."

Week 6

Be the hardest-working, not the smartest, person in the room.

"9 to 5"

—*Dolly Parton*

Life Lesson

This is yet another college story with a cool ending. Remember I said how difficult my college years were? It was so grueling to care for a new family, a working wife, a work study program that demanded way too much attention, and taking between eighteen to twenty-four credit hours per semester. If that were not enough, there was a supplemental academic program that was pointed out to me by a counselor, and he encouraged me to apply at the University of Oklahoma (OU), our intrastate rival school. We could attend as Oklahoma State students, funded by the state. The University of Oklahoma was where the cool kids attended. They were the "city kids" and drove better cars, and what you wore said everything about the neighborhood where you were raised.

If your essay qualified you to attend, the Scholar Leadership Enrichment Program (SLEP) was fully paid and allowed you to spend eight hours each day for a week with a world-renowned professor or businessperson. The class was only about twenty people. I was selected and attended two sessions in two separate weeks over that year on top of my impossible school schedule.

The second one was with Clarence "Kelly" Johnson, the leader of the "Skunk Works," a secret government think tank that built the U2 and the SR-71 spy planes. It was an amazing week. He told a story of the legendary test pilot Chuck Yeager taking the SR-71 up for a test flight, a 170,000-pound titanium jet, which hid from radar, flew at Mach 3, and had a camera that could take a picture of a golf ball from fifty thousand feet.

It was difficult to build a plane out of titanium (so it wouldn't melt at high speed) and have it go fast enough to have enough lift to keep it in the air. It was a true aeronautical engineering marvel. Well, I guess the engineers did too good of a job with the design for lift. When Yeager came around for a landing on the dry lake bed, the GE engines, operating at only idle speed, were enough to keep the airplane in the air.

It would not land. He had to cut the engines and let it drop, which he did well. Kelly Johnson died in December of 1990. I get to say I knew him.

I passed the courses and received two credit hours for each course. I missed a week of school, so there was much to do upon my return. This was doubly overwhelming, and again I was near a breaking point. After one of my engineering classes, I went to the front to greet the now late Dr. Don Adams. He was usually abrupt and gruff—not with me, though; he didn't sleep much, and his home life was not the best. He often slept in his office. I reached the front of the class, knowing I had missed a major exam while I was out, one of only three exams of the entire course. I had no idea how I was going to get ready to take that test in the usual two- or three-day time frame. "Doc," as we called him, knew that I was married and that I worked on a National Science Foundation work study, had a kid, was a good student, and never missed a class or a review session. The struggle was real. He could see it in my bloodshot eyes. Doc knew I was distinguishing myself by taking these extra opportunities to learn, but he had a class to run. I wasn't very smart when it came to engineering. I had to work extremely hard at it—harder than most. And I worked extremely hard.

I approached the podium and reminded him that I needed to set a time to take that test. Then this happened. Doc opened his grade book, paged to our class and looked down the list of names and grades for each person handwritten in neat engineering lettering. He ran his finger down through the B's to find Rodney Branch. He paused and looked over at me standing there. He said quietly, "Mr. Branch, you made a 94 percent on the last exam. I think that is what you made on this one too." He wrote "94" next to my name in the only empty square in the list of test scores. I don't know how many times I said thank you, I'm sure it was an obnoxious number, for that was a pure act of kindness. Except for Nona Cowan, no other person outside my family did more for my self-confidence and helped me understand the power of building relationships with deep caring.

You know the old saying from Maya Angelou, "People will forget what you said, people will forget what you did, but people will never forget how you made them feel." In my last conversation with Doc a few years ago, he was the oldest professor and oldest student at OSU at seventy-eight years old, still taking classes. He passed away a few years back. I will always remember how he made me feel that day. I was the hardest-working person in the room because I knew I wasn't the smartest one.

Week 7

Have the courage to accept a job you don't know how to do.

"Learning to Fly"

—Pink Floyd

Life Lesson

Let me take you back to 2014. I was sitting at a Kansas State graduation dinner in Manhattan, Kansas, celebrating with my oldest daughter who had just gotten her master's degree in industrial and organizational psychology. My wife and daughter leaned in conspiratorially, as if hatching a plot. "Rod," my daughter said, "you can do this." My wife nodded, "Seriously. You've got this." They were talking about me going back to school to get *my* master's.

At the time, I was working in HR for a large division of a nationwide industrial services company. I had a full plate negotiating union contracts in the most god-forsaken corners of inner-city ghettos and industrial complexes across the nation. But the more I thought about going back to school, the more intrigued I became. After researching programs that aligned with my career goals, I landed on pursuing a master's degree in global human resources management. Kansas State's program in organizational and industrial psychology also sounded solid. But then the University of Liverpool popped up, at a similar cost and with an international twist. That sealed it. If I was going to think globally, I might as well study globally. That decision lit a new fire in me. I thought, *Maybe I* should *work internationally while I'm studying internationally.*

About then, a smaller global tank manufacturer, whose leadership I knew, was looking for a head of HR. I threw my name in the ring. During the interview, the president, Paul, someone I'd known from my industrial days, looked at me and asked about payroll and benefits. I told him the truth: "I've never been in charge of payroll and benefits; however, I've been in the room when it was happening." He laughed and said, "Rod, we get people paid. It can't be that hard." Famous last words.

So I accepted the job as VP of HR, and within a couple of months, just as I was dipping my toe into the payroll waters and learning the difference between a W2 and a W9, there was a knock on my door. The CFO came in, looking pale. "Rod, we've got a situation," he said. The Department of Labor in Dallas had called. They were about to sue the company. Turns out, the DOL had already *been* to the office before I started there. With badges. They'd audited the 401(k) plan, had findings, issued compliance letters, and were waiting for a response. Our payroll manager, who came as a direct report to my new VP role, knew about the unannounced visit from the Feds and had not told even the CFO—no one knew! Then she threw away the warning letters—*unopened*. They are the letters that don't mince words or mess around. They have official raised-letter seals. It was every HR leader's version of a horror movie, this one called *I Know What You Didn't Do Last Summer!*

I was in over my head—only one month in. There it was. This must be what it is like in these C-suite jobs. There is a reason why it is not called a *C-sweet* job. I panicked. What I knew was we had to show some action, or the Feds were going to do it for us, and the outcome could not be managed in that case. I reached out to my benefits broker, who said they had a branch that did 401(k) work. He connected us, and they were the lifeline, the foothold, and the safety net I needed to get on a track to fix this. I don't think I slept for a long time.

I buried my fears and put my engineering hat on. I used the scientific method:

1. Define the problem.
2. Identify resources.
3. Know what is missing.
4. Guess accurately at the missing pieces.
5. Describe what success looks like.
6. Design a solution.
7. Execute.
8. Test.

First, I called the IRS agent in Dallas, introduced myself, admitted I was new to the job and was just discovering this problem. I committed to getting the right answer as fast as I could. I set about discovering all that could be wrong with the plan. In the process I found that we had no broker. I hired a broker. I called in outside auditors. The large 401(k) provider and partner had not cashed out people correctly, or matched correctly, or administered enrollees correctly. The albatross was the inability to analyze six years of data on green sheets of computer paper. Huh?

The payroll company delivered only PDF versions of reports on payroll runs. There was a closet stacked floor to ceiling with that continuous-form green bar printout paper—nothing digital you could put in Excel to do analysis. We had to go back six years. I fired the 401(k) provider. I fired the benefits broker, and I fired the payroll clerk. We rebuilt everything from the ground up. I was doing all of this for the first time—ever. Some of it was like blindly swinging for a pinata hanging from the ceiling of a dark garage. It took *two and a half years* to make it right. We combed through every PDF record, calculated every owed penny, and made sure every impacted employee was made whole. The DOL issued no fines because of our diligence to get it right.

There were many heroes in that story, but I might've walked away as the biggest winner. By the end of it, I didn't just *know* payroll and benefits. I had *lived* it. I learned how to swim in deep water because someone shoved me in. And somehow I surfaced—only with grayer hair.

This "life lesson" for me kept showing up on my career doorstep. Not long ago, I was moderating a panel of four powerhouse female CEOs in front of a packed ballroom of aspiring HR leaders, most of them women, leaning in, taking notes, and soaking up wisdom like sunlight. At the end of the session, I asked the panelists a question I love asking leaders. "What's one life lesson you'd offer to encourage this audience today?" Each had a gem. But one answer hit me right in the chest, because I'd lived it. She said simply, "Don't be afraid to take a job you don't know how to do." I've quoted her dozens of times since. Why? Because that's exactly how I ended up in one of the most challenging and growth-filled roles of my career.

I completed the degree program in December of 2016 and was offered a much larger job back at the company I had left three years earlier. I was much more HR-savvy after the experience with the Department of Labor.

So here's my advice, borrowed from that brilliant CEO: Take the job, even if you *are* afraid and especially if it sparks your curiosity.

You'll never feel 100 percent ready for your biggest opportunity. That's okay. Readiness is overrated. Courage is what counts.

Sometimes the best swimming lesson is getting tossed in the deep end.

Week 8

Keep a journal. Your future self will thank you.

"Write This Down"
—George Strait

Life Lesson

When we were raising our boys, we mostly stuck to the old script. You know the one. Boys don't cry. Boys don't keep diaries. Boys are hunters, not journalists. Stoic, not sensitive. Fixers, not feelers. Journaling? That was a "girl thing."

To be fair, our parents and grandparents were doing the best they could with what they knew. But somewhere along the way, after enough therapy, reflection, and coffee-fueled conversations, we started getting smarter about self-care. And when I found out that world leaders, philosophers, and Navy SEALs all keep journals? Well, I gave myself permission to drop the macho act and pick up a pen. And you know what? Journaling is powerful. It's cleansing. It's like writing one of those rage-filled emails where you tell someone *exactly* what you think, pour your entire soul onto the screen ... and then delete it. Just the act of writing sets you free. You didn't need to send it; you just needed to *say* it. That's journaling.

Julia Cameron, in her 1992 classic *The Artist's Way*, calls it "morning pages." Every day, she says, we should write three pages of stream-of-consciousness gobbledygook to clear the mental junk drawer.[4] She sees it as spiritual. I see it as survival. It's like prayer with grammar errors.

And if you think journaling has to be pretty? Anne Lamott wants a word. In *Bird by Bird*, she popularized the term *shitty first draft*, and it's exactly what it sounds like.[5] You don't write to impress anyone. You write to be free. And for folks like me, raised to believe feelings were to be managed, not expressed, the "shitty first draft" was a revelation. It meant I could write badly and still heal. In fact, *that was the point.*

I didn't come to journaling early. I came to it through detours: two marriages, four kids, three careers, a few academic grinds, and more than a dozen zip codes. I had a first wife who battled depression, long stretches where mentors were unavailable, and countless moments when even hours of therapy couldn't untangle the knot in my chest. Sometimes, despair didn't make an appointment. It just showed up. And when it did, journaling was one of the only places I could go. Funny thing is, I actually won a scholarship in high school for a national paper I wrote about people with disabilities. I liked writing. I was good at it. But I didn't follow that path. I took the "safe" route and became an engineer.

Now, engineering has its merits, but let's be honest, it's not known for nurturing emotional expression. While the arts majors were sipping espresso and finding themselves, we were grinding away on green grid paper, caffeinated and socially awkward. Writing didn't stand a chance. So I buried it. Writing, I mean. Because men didn't do that. We solved problems, built things, and moved on. Until we couldn't. Eventually, I rediscovered journaling, not as a career move, not as a creative outlet, but as a survival tool. A place to dump my negativity and stack my wins.

Motivational speaker André Young, whom I met at a breakfast meeting a year or so ago, gave me this gem: "End each day by writing down one win." Writing it down makes it real. That one little practice? Life-changing. Because journaling isn't just a place to vent. It's where we *sort* things. It's where we *store* the victories and *release* the regret. It's not a diary. It's a conversation, with yourself, your future, and maybe even your faith. So no, journaling isn't just for girls. It's for humans. If you've never tried it, here's your invitation: Grab a notebook, pour a cup of whatever soothes you, and just start writing. It doesn't matter what. It doesn't matter how well. Just begin. Your first draft will be terrible. And that's exactly what makes it great. Journaling is like a disposal for your frustrations that sits next to your safe that contains all your precious memories.

Week 9

Be curious, not judgmental.

"Teach Your Children"

—Crosby, Stills, Nash, and Young

Life Lesson

I became a fan of *Ted Lasso* in exactly the opposite way I could barely stand to watch *The Office*. *The Office* was a collection of the most dysfunctional, stereotypical employees you could cram into a corporate setting. From my corporate human resources leadership seat, I couldn't help but see HR and leadership violations in almost every episode. My brain wanted to jump in, "Let's address this productively!" But of course, they did not do so; they doubled down and made it worse. Some hospital work environments are the same, and I can't say how I know that secondhand.

Ted Lasso, on the other hand, felt like leadership therapy. Episode after episode, there were insights—little moments that showed leadership principles at work in believable, human ways. Take the dart scene. Ted is underestimated, dismissed, and bet against. He reveals he was bullied as a kid—not because people knew him but because they didn't. They never got curious. They just assumed and judged.

It reminded me of a conversation I had years ago with Stephen M. R. Covey, son of *The 7 Habits* author, Stephen Covey. In his book *The Speed of Trust*, Stephen M. R. Covey points out that we judge others by their behavior and judge ourselves by our intent.[6] That hit me hard. We hear tones, see word choice, notice body language, and instantly form an opinion. But our interpretation is filtered through our own damaged antennae—our past experiences, old stories, and lingering insecurities.

Don Miguel Ruiz says in *The Four Agreements* to "not take anything personally."[7] Often, what others say or do has more to do with *their* reality than a deliberate intent to harm you. And the reverse is true—our own words and behaviors may land very differently than we intended.

The key is to pause when we feel stung by something—a comment in a meeting, an email that rubs us the wrong way, even a text. Instead of reacting instantly, ask, *Am I judging their behavior or trying to understand their intent? Could my reaction be more about me than them?*

One practical trick? If you feel the urge to fire back an emotional email, go ahead and write it all out, no holding back. Then step away for a day. When you come back, ask yourself, *Will this make things better or worse?* Ninety-nine times out of a hundred, you'll hit delete. You'll have processed the emotion without burning a bridge. You just needed an emotional cleansing.

In my early career days, my first boss got fired and another person took over. I was the newest and youngest engineer. Several of the older engineers, who knew that the fired boss and I were friends, hated my old boss and took it out on me. They would come up with some lame excuse every weekend so that I had to cover their weekend work—spending all weekend standing on a rig floor in Western Oklahoma with the wind howling through my cheap vendor-giveaway jacket. Since I was not a particularly good engineer, I took it on the chin. There was no email back then, but I did sit and write a letter with my 0.5mm Pentel mechanical pencil and a green gridded engineering pad. I went deep into how unfair that was, especially when I had very young children. It was hard to work all day every day and not see them grow up. I had that with my dad, and that just added to the sting. Each sentence was carefully lettered with the fine mechanical drawing style that was burned into me in drafting class. Each lowercase letter became a capital letter, and each capital letter was just a larger version of the other letters. I wore out the green engineering pad as the eraser tore through the first page many times in my multiple drafts. I spilled years of pent-up emotions, constantly clicking the Pentel as I asked for more pencil lead to continue writing. I carried that letter for weeks before deciding that it would do me no good to rock the boat. I tossed it.

Managing our own emotions is much easier said than done. Being self-aware is another. Often it takes our best friend at work or a trusted accountability partner who sees us often and who is willing to show us how our comments are landing with people. We need the unvarnished truth to be able to change. Flip Flippen told me once that we need an emotionally compelling reason to make personal changes.
As Ted would say, "Barbecue sauce." The surface flavor might get your attention, but the real truth is what's underneath. And before we judge, it's worth asking, What do we actually know for sure?

Week 10

Know your personal brand, values, and purpose.

"Man in the Mirror"
—*Michael Jackson*

Life Lesson

After high school, I often felt like a steel ball in a pinball machine—bounced around by life without much control over where I'd land. By nineteen, I suddenly had an instant family, and the world was no longer my oyster. I was in survival mode. I buried my shame under relentless work. In a tough job market, I landed an engineering job. Then came the pressure to prove I belonged there. That's hard to do when you secretly hate the work and when, truth be told, you're not particularly good at it. I moved wherever they told me to move, climbing slowly through the ranks: Engineer I, Engineer II, Engineer III. Each promotion was just a new number after my name—same work, just harder.

Everything changed when they asked me to take on a lobbying role. For the first time, I saw that I had choices beyond engineering—roles I could do and maybe even enjoy. Later I joined the HR team at Enron. I didn't ask for the job; I just took it. And for the first time in my career, I liked what I was doing.

Years later, at an industrial services company, I finally got the VP title—after my wife encouraged me to ask for it. But at first, the title was all I had. I didn't really know how to add value at the VP level. Then, with the encouragement of my wife and daughters, I enrolled in graduate school. There, I experienced an epiphany. I learned how to merge business goals with the philosophy of motivating people. I discovered "caring" and saw how it was the cornerstone of all great leadership. I just wish I'd had the courage to see and believe in myself earlier.

My friend Liz Townsend was the first to put it into words. A group she introduced me to reinforced it. After I sat in as a guest on their presentations and gave feedback, they recalled my visit weeks later and said, "Rod's brand is caring."

I'd always considered myself a caring person, and then I began to notice how it showed up in my work and life. Unsolicited feedback confirmed it. People told me they felt seen when I leaned in and listened intently. A grieving team could see the care in my eyes when I spoke after they had lost a colleague to suicide. A widow of an employee who had died unexpectedly told me she felt cared for. My team members, whom I cannot pay enough for all they do, tell me they stay because they feel safe to learn, to make mistakes, and to grow. So, once challenged that I had a brand of caring, I suppose I could see it.

So how do you discover your own brand? It is about uncovering the most authentic, valuable, and consistent version of yourself, the "you" that others experience every day.

You can start with a conversation with yourself: What do I respect most in others? What was I doing the last time a day flew by? For what do people consistently come to me seeking? On what topics do people ask my opinion? What energizes me? What drains me? What truths and core values will I never compromise?

If you try this, get feedback. If you asked twenty colleagues, friends, family, to give two or three words that describe you, what words would be repeated most often? Those are your brand clues. Think about your habits and the moments that define you:

> **For what are you known?** Are you the answer person in your field of expertise? Are you a great negotiator or consensus driver?
>
> **What do you stand for?** Are there causes or movements you represent as part of your values?
>
> **What are the memorable statements or quotes people attribute to you?** These are the things that outlive your time on Earth.

Your brand lives at the intersection of what you are good at and what you love doing. That's a powerful corner to stand on—an excellent location, location, location to build your life's work.

Week 11

Be someone your younger self would be proud of.

"Forever Young"
—*Rod Stewart*

Life Lesson

If you've ever driven south on I-45 in Houston, just outside downtown, you've seen the railroad bridge with "Be Someone" painted in bold graffiti colors across the black steel. Since 2012, it's been there off and on. Protest slogans come and go, painted under the cover of night, and someone always changes it back to *Be Someone*.

The message, at least for me, is this: *Be someone your younger self would be proud of*. And also, *Be someone to someone*.

I'm not talking about being someone to someone only in the big, milestone moments, but rather, on the daily. Be someone in how you treat people, in the values you live out, in the way you handle yourself when nobody's watching. Think about the younger you—less wise, less experienced, maybe a little naive. Would they look at you now and think, *Yeah, that's who I want to be when I grow up*?

A lot of what looks like wisdom is just having lived long enough to know how the story ends because you've made the mistakes. Looking back, what would you do differently now? Had I been able to see around the corner just a bit, I might have made different choices. More importantly for me now is, how do those moments cause me to choose differently? And what am I doing differently now based on past mistakes?

I was at happy hour recently with a friend—someone I think of as a daughter. She's Hispanic, brilliant, and beautiful. Life didn't hand her anything. She powered through three years of mechanical engineering before switching to political science at the University of Houston. Then she put herself through law school, passed the Texas bar on her first try, then passed the California bar—no small feat, even for the financially and socially advantaged.

Now she's the youngest trial attorney at her firm, and in her first ninety days she zeroed in on every criticism from her senior partners—boomers with plenty of opinions. She'd built a mental framework where every piece of feedback reinforced the idea that she had to outwork every man just to keep up—just to stay even.

I told her, "Let's look at this a different way. Those criticisms are gold. They're your greatest learning opportunity. Cherish them. They're shaping you into the attorney your younger self could never have imagined." It is a tough pill to swallow, especially if you have clawed your way just to have this amazing opportunity. You might ask, "Do I have to continue clawing even after I have 'made it'?"

I get the chip-on-the-shoulder thing. I was a young dad, unplanned. I felt judged. I'd wanted to go to law school, and my first real high school love married one of my best friends, who became the lawyer I thought I'd be. (Ouch. Maybe I'm not over that yet.)

Years later, I apologized to my dad for not listening to his "birds and bees" talk. I apologized for derailing his plan and my own plan. He said, "But you worked hard to right yourself. Look where you are now."

"Be proud. Regret little. See the good," he said. There are always things your younger self didn't know you could do, and you never know what you can do next.

So, *be someone*. Every day. Because someday, your younger self is going to look back at you and either nod in pride ... or shake their head..

Week 12

Time is both the kindest and the cruelest of all life's dimensions.

"Turn! Turn! Turn!"
—*The Byrds*

Life Lesson

Let's pretend you're 40 years old. Okay, some of you are not pretending. Studies say the average book buyer is somewhere between 32 and 43, so you're safely in the club. Statistically, you've got 1.62 children, and for kindness's sake, let's round up and make that second child a whole person. You're welcome.

Now, in my case, two of my actual whole-person children live in Seattle. Between their trips here and ours there, we see each other about three times a year. My life expectancy, according to the charts, is 83. I'm 67 now. If we're playing the averages, that leaves me 16 years. But let's be realistic: Travel gets harder with age, so let's say the clock on my "active travel years" runs out around 80. That leaves 13 years of seeing my kids three times a year. That's 39 more visits.

Thirty-nine. That's not a lot. I will see my CEO more than that in two months' time.

So, let's talk bucket lists. Got places you've dreamed of going? Surfing in Hawaii, skiing in the Alps, hiking Machu Picchu, braving the Sahara? Here's the truth—your tolerance for extreme weather and bone-rattling adventures drops faster than a cell phone battery at 1 percent. And those late nights "oonsing" at the neon-lit club until two a.m.? Yeah, that's going to morph into sipping tea and watching the Weather Channel until ten.

My advice? Rank your bucket list from "requires a Sherpa" to "requires a patio chair," and do the hard stuff while you're still young enough to bend over without making noises. Save the Tuscan balcony with a glass of wine (or fine bourbon) for the grand finale.

Make the time with loved ones count. On my fiftieth birthday, my older son asked Lou Holtz—one of my favorite coaches and human beings—if he'd write me a note. Lou wrote, "Rod, don't count the years, make the years count." I know he didn't invent that phrase, but he meant it, and it rings truer every day.

My sister is eight years younger than I am. When I left home at eighteen, she was ten. Decades later, she wrote me a birthday letter saying she regretted me not being around during her high school years—missing her in her prom dress, missing moments we'll never get back. That hit me hard. Time is selfish. It doesn't care how much you want it to slow down.

Recently, holding my newest grandchild—likely the only one to carry the Branch name another generation—I found myself reluctant to let go when it was time to drop them at the airport. That's the emotional gravity of time. You can't make more of it. You can't buy it. You can only use it ... or lose it.

My dad paid for all of us to go on a cruise for their fiftieth wedding anniversary. We were all going for the "free" food, the drinks, the entertainment. My parents were going for the memory of all the kids and grandkids around one dinner table three times a day—except that one day my underage nephew got into some grog and missed most of the next day.

It's The Old Course Swilcan Bridge story. It wasn't about the golf. It was about the experience of a father and a son. It was Pebble Beach and the old-fashioneds around the fire pit as the bagpiper marched off the course at dusk. It had nothing to do with the golf. The value was in the life we lived those days.

This weekend is my grandson's first birthday in Seattle. That is a long way from Houston—like the upper left corner of the map. My wife is still recovering from cancer surgery and still needs some help, and I have to be in California on business the following week. But it's his *first* birthday. But my wife needs me here. There is only one *first* birthday. I mentioned it to Reneé and she insisted I go. It is about the memories. She gets it too.

Now I get why my grandparents cried when we pulled out of their driveway after visits. I get why my dad used to say, "It's just like a tonic when you come by." Back then, a tonic was pitched as a miracle cure. Today, it'd probably be a THC drink or a nineteenth-century recipe for Coca-Cola with actual cocaine in it. Either way, the feeling was the same—it made him feel better.

So here's my challenge to you: Stop gifting "stuff" that will end up in a closet someday. Gift experiences. Maximize the time. Make the memories. Because memories are the only things time can't take away. Your legacy is how you left them feeling. If you have to leave them, leave them feeling good about your time together.

Week 13

Don't underestimate the human spirit.

"Eye of the Tiger"
—*Survivor*

Life Lesson

Wallace Branch, no middle name, my grandfather, was born in 1904 in a farmhouse in Many, Louisiana (pronounced "Manny"). He likely entered the world on the kitchen table, as was common in the tough times of the rural South. One of twelve children, Wallace grew up under the weight of poverty and expectation as part of a sharecropping family. If you're unfamiliar with sharecropping, here's how it worked. You lived on someone else's land rent-free if you worked their farm. If the crop "made," you owed nothing. If it didn't, you had to pay the landowner the difference in cash, a commodity they never had.

Wallace's father was a Baptist preacher first and a farmer second. Family legend says that in one of his best years, he earned just twenty-four dollars preaching. He allegedly treated his children like indentured servants, refusing to let them leave the farm. Wallace dropped out of school in the third grade to work the land. He used to retell his proudest story over and over that he could recite his multiplication tables better than anyone in that third grade class. Looking back, I see that repetition for what it was: the echo of a man wrestling with impostor syndrome, honest ignorance, and the stress of uncertainty. His multiplication tables were his proof that he was enough.

Eventually, Wallace found the courage to leave the farm. With a third grade education and little knowledge of the world beyond the cattle guard, he packed up his wife, their few belongings, and their two kids, and fled to DeRidder, Louisiana. He took whatever work he could find—milk truck driver, dump truck driver helping build Fort Polk, produce manager, even running a small country store on the town's edge.

After WWII, he purchased two side-by-side wooden apartments from a decommissioned Air Force base on the edge of DeRidder. He moved them to a suburban lot, propped them up on blocks, converted a closet into a rudimentary bathroom with marine paint, and moved in. He began renting out the extra rooms to travelers. People did that sort of thing in the '40s and '50s—resourceful, legal, just barely enough to get by. Interestingly, after the Depression and while running his country store, my grandfather didn't trust banks. He kept all his store money under the bed in paper bags.

That survival instinct propelled him. It passed to my dad and down to me. Branch boys become scrappers, driven by hardship, whether inherited or self-inflicted. My dad started with nothing and became a professional engineer. I started with a shovel in Western Kansas. I was working as a roustabout, digging holes looking for underground leaks near storage tanks while the pumper napped in the shade.

Wallace was motivated by socioeconomic discrimination. And it follows that my dad was placed in a lower academic track simply because he came from the country—assumed to be ignorant. He didn't complain much. We don't complain. We don't quit. We fight. There is much more about our stories throughout this book. It is resilience, the kind Dr. Taryn Marie encourages. Dr. Taryn Marie wrote *The 5 Practices of Highly Resilient People*, which inspired me to write some vulnerable stories online. A few trusted colleagues implored me to write this book after reading the stories. Then in somewhat of a Hail Mary, I asked Dr. Taryn Marie if she would write the foreword for this book and she graciously agreed.

Starting out my adult life hungry (literally), hopeful, and disadvantaged by my own doing, I find it hard to relate to people who groan about coming into the office to work. Let's see. A roustabout moving pipe in the 115-degree heat of the southeastern New Mexico sand hills, or a padded chair and chilly air conditioning crunching numbers and doing hand (not CAD) technical drawings. For us, it was never "I have to go to work." It was always "I get to." Survivalists don't take opportunities for granted. Every paycheck is a victory.

The reason we can't trace the Branch history is that no one ever had any money. Typically, in the Branch line, there were multiple generations living under one roof. Often the census asked for only the name of the head of the household, and how many and what gender and age the residents were. So many went unrecorded by name. The ancestry trail dies into an impoverished dead end.

It's been fifty-three years since I earned my first paycheck, ringing a Salvation Army bell at Christmas in Oklahoma City. I stood in a freezing wind for three hours straight each day, miserable, yes, and proud. It was my job. Someone was counting on me. Someone always has. From sharecropper roots, roustabout dangers and discipline, and drinking coffee using rig water and a paper towel for a filter after being up for seventy-two hours straight, it was work. I was glad to have it. Scrapper. Resilient.

Never underestimate the drive of the human spirit.

Week 14

Your best is the best you can do.

"Let It Be"

—The Beatles

Life Lesson

Everyone needs at least one good friend at work. They're the ones who'll give you a ride when your car's in the shop, notice when you're having a rough day, swing by your desk in the morning to ask about your weekend, and share a coffee just because.

For me, that guy is Darryl.

Darryl's in his fifties. Like me, he's an average-size man, which means we tend to notice how tall everyone else is. His build isn't particularly athletic, so when he walked into my office one day and announced, "I'm training for an Ironman," I almost spit my coffee.

For the uninitiated, an Ironman—clearly invented by a masochist—is a race that starts with a 2.4-mile swim, followed with a 112-mile bike ride, and ends with a 26.2-mile marathon. In one day. Though Darryl was moderately athletic, no one would've bet on him for this kind of Everest. But he'd been reading inspiring stories about paraplegic and otherwise physically disadvantaged athletes who had conquered the Ironman. Then he thought, *Why not me?*

He hired a coach, built a training schedule, and committed. Almost every day for a year, he ran, biked, and swam. He survived a few wipeouts on the bike. He pushed through brutal ten-mile runs in the South Texas heat—weather that could knock the wind out of you just walking to the mailbox. After each practice session, he'd tell me his new personal best, followed by, "I'm going to have to do better than that if I want to finish."

And here's the thing, as most Ironman competitors will tell you: For many the goal is simply to finish. Darryl trained like a man possessed. His coach taught him swimming cadence, running techniques, bike positions, and pacing strategies. He was building stamina and resilience, not just chasing a stopwatch.

The family sacrifice was no small thing either. Training at that level eats hours from your week like Pac-Man, and you need your family's full support to keep at it.

Then came race day: 2024, Houston, Texas. Hot. Humid. Windy. The kind of day you wouldn't wish on your lawn, much less your body. Darryl crushed the swim, well under the cutoff time, and hit the bike course looking strong. But once he cleared the sheltered streets of The Woodlands and hit the open highway tollway, it was like pedaling through molasses. The wind on the overpasses pushed back like it had a personal grudge. As the miles dragged on, it became clear he was flirting with the bike cutoff time. And eventually, the clock won—he timed out and was disqualified. Seriously, that is just unfair. That moment for him had to have been devastating. I could feel it in my chest for him.

Later, a friend of mine, Somer, who worked at the race asked me how Darryl did. When I told her he'd timed out on the bike, she shook her head and said, "A lot of people did. The wind was the worst it's ever been. No shame in that." Then she paused and added something I'll never forget: "You know, Rod, it's not all about race day. They should give a medal for the year of training, the aches, and pains of getting in shape in your fifties, the time away from family, the discipline. The real value is in the training. You learn a lot about yourself. You spend a lot of time with yourself."

She was right. The real prize isn't just the finish line; it's everything you gain on the way there. The discipline. The resilience. The self-discovery. Darryl didn't cross the line that day, but the victory was already his. When you've done your best, be satisfied that you left it all on the field. Because sometimes, the race you think you're running isn't the one that matters most.

Week 15

Accept the things you cannot change.

"Que Sera, Sera (Whatever Will Be, Will Be)"
—*Doris Day*

Life Lesson

I was the newly named CHRO of a three-thousand-person company. It was the biggest job I had ever had and had been hired back for the top job after having had a lower-level HR role before. When I accepted, I showed up to the familiar Houston Galleria area high-rise and my large office with a nice conference table. I had a grin as wide as Texas. I was proud of what I had achieved, fresh out of graduate school, armed with knowledge and courage for the first time. We were in the middle of some of the best lunch spots in Houston, where the lunch crowd was full of brand-touting polos, boat shoes, seersucker, and short tennis skirts with $5,000 handbags. Coming from a manufacturing plant, it was like Dorothy's first day in technicolor Oz! Within weeks, the CEO came to my office to tell me we were acquiring our biggest competitor and that I was going to be the CHRO of the now six-thousand-employee business.

Running HR for a huge company was great news. The synergies of the companies were something of a matchmaker. There were plenty of opportunities to consolidate back-office operations and look at more practical office space than in the ritzy area of Houston's Galleria. The economic synergy adds value to the bottom line overnight. Economic synergies are the life blood of acquisitions. Back-office functions are combined to save money, and sometimes entire offices are combined for the sake of efficiency. The acquired company's office space is in Deer Park, Texas, in the industrial ship channel area of Houston. Not a garden spot, and unless you are from there, you would never choose to travel there or probably ever stumble upon it. You could see the area on the horizon from our western suburb skyscraper location, so it didn't look too far. The news that we were relocating from the shiny Galleria of Houston to the less prestigious ship channel riddled with refineries and industrial complexes was troubling.

The first thing I noticed about the new office was the commute. My forty-five minutes to Houston's version of Rodeo Drive was now twice that one way. People say everything in Houston is an hour away from everything else, even if you can see it from where you're sitting. But okay, let's do this. I'll crank out a little earlier and put on audiobooks to fill my day with education. This is the price one might pay to be at the position I was proud to have. Every job has challenges, and the commute to work shouldn't be one of them. The curb appeal of this job is something of a Hollywood real estate show.

I also noticed the scenery on the drive to work had changed. How could I not notice? I was no longer approaching the office each morning through beautiful glass towers, green city parks, and bustling high-end shopping centers the likes of Wilshire Boulevard and Fifth Avenue. My route took me on SH 225. It is said 225 is the most dangerous stretch of highway in the world. With gasoline and crude oil storage tanks lining the frontage roads on both sides for eight miles, one ill-placed Cessna mayday and half of Houston would be separated from the rest of the city. The view was entirely industrial: refineries, chemical plants, and a web of train tracks. The glass towers of the Galleria gave way to smokestacks belching burn-off flares from the refineries, and the pedestrians were no longer wearing Armani suits, cashmere coats, and designer hats but rather grease-stained Levi's, bright orange safety vests, and yellow hard hats. The smells had changed. The air that used to be filled with the warm, sweet temptations from artisan bakeries and the spicy sauces and smoking meat of nearby restaurants now reeked of the acrid stench of sulfur and the punch in the nose of burning tires.

All the nuances of the new gig started out okay. The days were long, but I had an opportunity to make a significant impact. I got invited to join some of the larger and more prestigious networking groups for large corporations. Speaking engagements on my leadership model came quickly and to very cool locations.

The commute soon became a grind. I had some well-placed impostor syndrome, and I should have been able to manage this role well enough, but I wasn't quite ready for it. I wasn't getting along with the CFO; she was entrenched in the old manual ways of payroll and wanted to keep it that way. I learned later that no one was getting along with this person—it wasn't just me. Also, learning and development was a growing part of the role and I had little background in field training—nor did I have great interest. I was well versed in leadership development, but there was less interest in that, even though it was desperately needed.

Just as I was getting used to early-morning and late-evening commutes and windows rolled up on beautiful days during my long trips to and from the office, my mother got really sick and ultimately ended up in the hospital. We didn't know it at the time, but she would live there and then a rehab hospital inpatient for a total of five months. My dad would sit with her for eight hours every day, bored out of his mind. If she ever got to go home, she would be totally dependent on others—my dad and me. As I have and will describe even more in this book, tragedy brings loneliness and separation from friends who don't know what to say or do, so they do nothing. Those you think will come visit rarely come, and when they do, they leave sooner than you are ready. During those five months, I focused on my dad. It is usually the caregiver who gives out before the patient. He looked forward to steak night each week with me at a local brewery away from the sterile stench of Clorox and urine, and looked forward to me showing up many nights and staying until the hospital visiting hours ended.

This new wrinkle of caregiver's caregiver required a few more hours in my day. This Tetris puzzle of trying to be at the hospital when the doctor came by and then when Dad needed to get dinner required getting up even earlier for my trek to the ship channel and leaving a little earlier to get home.

Some days I would meet with the doctor with my parents at seven thirty in the morning and get to work before nine. But I would have to leave by four p.m. to get to the hospital by six if I wanted to see my mom that day. These octogenarians can be a lot of work. Once at home in the evenings, I had to muster the energy to catch up on all that I missed at work during those hours—and those were hours no one witnessed. I had to sleep fast during that time. Coffee, prayer, and motivational audiobooks got me through the days.

The spirit was willing, but the flesh was weak. I was nodding off on my commutes home. I was a zombie at work. I was failing at everything at work *and* at home except being what my mom and dad needed.

I admit that I was underpowered for the job, willing to learn, but mostly just exhausted all the time. I was gaining weight, and when my mom died two years later, I was 208 pounds on this five-nine frame. I was not well emotionally or physically and felt like I had no one in my corner. I was not excited about anything, and all I wanted to do was pull back. It was a lonely place to be. I was failing and I knew it.

At the first opportunity, the CEO let me go. That's a polite way of saying I was fired. I was "let go." I don't blame him, and I think we are still friends. He characterized it as a "layoff," but I've seen this movie before—only, in the other movies, I was the one in the director's chair, and it was the other guy who was packing a box.

I decided that maybe until this COVID thing blew over, while I regained my health and glued together the shattered pieces of my ego, I should do consulting. So I did. My mom hung on, but my dad had to hire all-day help for her when she finally went home. The person we hired required a deposit of $1,300 up front in a direct deposit to her bank. The deposit would be applied to the last bill. When my mom died, we contacted her to say we no longer needed her and that we needed to collect back the deposit since we had not used her in five months. That was the last communication we made to her. Her phone no longer worked, and emails went unanswered. No one knew where she lived. It made sense now why she was changing phone numbers every other month. She stole that money from my parents.

I was empty. I was lonely. I think this was the first time since college that I was at my emotional and physical limits. Even the Alaskan Arctic had nothing on sick parents, a hard job, and three-plus hours of commuting each day to and from a less than desirable workplace. Sometimes, all you can do is to believe in hope and accept that there are things you cannot change.

Week 16

As Confucius said, "Don't strive to be well known; strive to be worth knowing".

"You've Got a Friend"
—James Taylor

Life Lesson

Life's lessons tend to come to me in threes. Marcus Buckingham was the first who introduced me to this important lesson: "People don't love companies they work for. They love the people they work with." Then, while watching a YouTube commencement speech, I heard Pastor Rick Warren preach that no one on their deathbed asks to see their diploma again. They ask for their people. And I saw Peyton Manning being asked about the highlight of his Hall of Fame career. I was not surprised by his answer. He did not mention the rings. Not the records. Not the Super Bowls. Can you guess the red thread tying these ideas together?

Let me tell you about a time when this week's lesson moved from philosophical to magical. It was mid-September 1992. I had just stepped into my first real Washington, DC, lobbying job where my job title wasn't "that gearhead from engineering who helps us explain complicated stuff to legislative assistants." It actually said "Director of Government Affairs" on my business card. No senior handlers. No safety net. Just me, a legal pad, and the pressure to look like I knew what I was talking about. There is something you need to know that happened a month earlier that changed the trajectory of my influence as a lobbyist.

From August 17 through August 20, I volunteered at the 1992 Republican National Convention (RNC) in Houston. At the big volunteer orientation meeting, after committing to work every day at the Astrodome doing *something*, one of the Secret Service agents decided I looked responsible enough, and I was put in charge of volunteer security at the RNC VIP entrance. I dutifully showed up every day in my white RNC volunteer T-shirt and took instructions from the Secret Service. That's where I met Fred. He was a tall, calm, quiet Secret Service agent who was otherwise quite normal-looking with a dry sense of humor and a badge that spoke of decades of public service at stratospheric levels. We struck up a friendship. He told stories of his "glamorous" life as a Secret Service agent. He told of how he rode in a C-130 cargo plane from Washington, DC, to Houston staring at the side of a presidential limousine while sitting on a wooden bench. He told me how unromantic his life had been and that he was staying at some fleabag "motel" on I-45 in North Houston in a neighborhood you wouldn't let your cat roam. Wow, that really isn't how the Secret Service is portrayed in the movies.

I had a volunteer team running the magnetometers, checking the dignitaries including the likes of Senator Bob Dole, Wynona Judd, Tanya Tucker, Senator Jack Kemp, Mama Ninfa Laurenzo, Pat Buchanan, and Senator Strom Thurmond. We had to check for weapons, Zippo lighters, and loose change. Over our five days together, Fred and I exchanged contact information and some Secret Service and RNC swag. I figured I'd never see him again. It was a fantastic way to start my new job having gotten close to some of the everyday Washington people.

Twenty-six days later, I'm on my first trip to Washington, DC, at my new job. I was asked to join the president of a division of our huge company and a group of execs for dinner with their spouses. I was still trying to remember where my hotel was when, over dinner, the president casually leaned over and said, "Our wives want to tour the White House tomorrow. Can you make that happen?" The words hung over his head like a cartoon bubble. Startled and panicked, trying to look hopeful and helpful to my new colleagues, I said, "Of course!" I had no idea why that came out of my face at that moment. I had no way to do that.

Now, even though this was before 9/11, to get into the White House for a tour, you had to go through a grueling process of getting a letter from your congressperson or camp out all day and brave the elements of a mile-long line that wound its way among the "unhoused" in the nearby parks, streets, and walkways. There was no way I could get that congressional wheel to turn before the group had to return to Houston. An internal panic set in. I barely had a subway pass, much less a way to pull off a coup to get five women into the White House on a whim. And just then, I remembered Fred. It was like a vision. A miracle. Or medieval painting of the Second Coming! What I didn't tell you is that Secret Service Agent Fred had shared with me in between credential checks and heat strokes that his "day job" was managing White House access. As in, he decided who got through the gate.

Was it too soon to ask a favor of someone like Fred, a person I liked and respected? I took a deep breath, dialed the number in my little black book of contacts for "Fred at the White House" (yes, that one). Fred picked up. After exchanging humble niceties, I told him the situation, expecting a polite, "Nice try, you unconnected, lobbyist impostor." Instead, he said, "Get me their full names, driver's license numbers, and Social Security numbers. I'll take care of it. I will call you in the morning with detailed instructions on how this all works."

The next morning, Fred called.

Before you could say "Who are those high-class ladies?" those socialites, dressed in their best Jackie-O, Oleg Cassini-channeling skirts, scarfs, and pumps were escorted past the sweaty line of hands-on-their-hips onlookers who were wondering what dignitaries were being paraded past them. They walked right into the White House's "Special Tour" escorted by men with shiny badges, black suits, and squiggly little wires connected to their ears. Those ladies pranced like they owned the place while I sat back, looking like a Washington insider with VIP connections. I wasn't. I just had a friend named Fred with whom I had built a value-based relationship.

That one incident in my first month at this new company earned me more trust and credibility than any policy memo or talking point ever could. Why? Because relationships matter. Buckingham, Warren, and Manning were trying to tell us. It's relationships! Not in a cheesy, "network your way to the top" kind of way. Rather, in a *genuine* way. And over time, I've realized that my most important accomplishments aren't listed on a résumé. They're the networking contacts, friendships, family members, and people just outside the chalk circle who show up when it matters. It isn't about popularity. It's about being someone who's worth knowing because people understand that to you, people matter more than power. Because when the trophies gather dust, *relationships last*.

So, build them. Guard them. Laugh with them. You never know when someone will need a lifeline.

Or when you will.

Part II – Resilient Leadership

Finding Your Strength in the Storm

Leadership isn't tested when everything is going right. It's tested when the plans fall apart—when what you thought you knew is replaced by what you're meant to learn. Resilient leadership lives in those moments. It's the ability to stay grounded when the ground itself shifts.

This section explores how caring, perseverance, and perspective shape our capacity to endure. It reminds us that resilience is not about never falling—it's about standing up differently each time. It's in the wreckage and the chaos where strength is revealed, in the waiting where optimism is born, and in the caring where courage takes root.

True leadership is less about control and more about calm. It's the steady voice that says, "You can do hard things," even when no one is listening—*especially* when no one is listening.

Week 17

Resilience reveals itself in the wreckage.

"Stronger (What Doesn't Kill You)"
—*Kelly Clarkson*

Life Lesson

It was June 1977 in Ness City, Kansas. Yes, that is a place. It is another one you have to be aiming for to pass through. It's not a destination; it is a bus stop. The sun was so hot it felt like you could hear it. I was nineteen years old, covered in oil field grime, working as a roustabout, basically one rung above a chain gang, only with worse coffee and no uniforms. Life was moving. This was my summer job, and back at school I was a double major in economics and sociology on a full-ride scholarship. Law school was the goal. The future looked bright enough to need shades.

Then the phone rang—the black one with the spiral cord, sitting on a table and weighing several pounds. I picked it up, not knowing that in the next thirty seconds, my entire life would explode. Her voice was shaky, and there was no mistaking the gravity: "We're having a baby. We need a plan." There was a long pause as if my video call had frozen the screen, then ... *boom!* That one sentence lit a match to everything I thought I knew. My old life, and my carefully charted course, burst into flames. Law school? Gone. Prestige? Vaporized. I could almost hear the scholarship funds being sucked into the vortex of shattered prosperity. There was no dramatic music, no Hollywood montage. We were now just two scared kids staring down adulthood with nothing but a divining rod, a broken compass, and a watch stuck on "Failure."

I was really scared. Scared in the way you see people curled up in the corner unable to form an intelligible sentence. I tried to share with my field boss the tragic news. He said, "So you got your girl all knocked up, did you?" It was not what I needed to hear. It put me in a class of icehouse nomads with a slight criminal record and mild drug addiction. This was not me. Please wake me from this nightmare.

But here's the part no one sees coming: We didn't run. We didn't crumble. We dug deep and then rose like a phoenix crawling out of the ashes with tuition bills in one hand and diaper coupons in the other. I traded pre-law for petroleum engineering technology. Not because it was glamorous but because it was practical. We needed money. We needed a future. I needed to finish school in a hurry. I took twenty-four credit hours one semester, because apparently, insanity and desperation make great bedfellows. We savored boxes of off-brand mac and cheese like it was gourmet. Every day I felt like I was pushing a wheelbarrow of bricks uphill like some desperate teenage version of Sisyphus. Days and nights were long. My wife at the time worked at the local grocery store in the office. We swapped off taking care of the baby. I was not good at engineering, so my nights were filled with short sleeps and long division. No computers—just a rudimentary calculator and lots of green engineering paper. We traveled every summer to some godforsaken part of the country, working in the oil fields, traveling in a tired 1964 Nova with 440 air conditioning. That's four windows rolled down and going at least forty miles per hour.

It was a grind. No vacations. No dinners out. No movie theaters. Just a twelve-inch black-and-white TV and the entertainment of a toddler. Changing majors after my freshman year and having few of my credit hours apply to engineering, I had to take more classes than the average student. I finished with honors in December 1980. Four and a half years and 167 credit hours (only 125 were required to graduate). We crossed that finish line. I graduated. I walked straight into a job with the company that would become BP. And that baby boy? That so-called detour? He's now a forty-seven-year-old success story, standing tall in life.

That moment, that phone call on the black desk phone, what felt like the *end* of everything, was actually the ignition point. The fire revealed a resolve I didn't know I had. Dr. Taryn Marie, in *The Five Practices of Highly Resilient People*, says we're forever changed when we pass through the narrow gates of adversity.[8] And she's right. You're not just tougher, you're *different*. Resilience rewrites your DNA. Matthew McConaughey calls these turning points, these unpredictable intersections in life, "greenlights." They are the pivot points in your life that you either contrive yourself or are ambushed by when you aren't looking. I call them "fire starters." Either way, those moments that nearly break us often remake us. Stronger. Sharper. Braver. A little charred around the edges, a few scars here and there, but deeply alive.

Your turning point might not be as dramatic as mine. Maybe your phoenix moment came after a layoff. A divorce. A diagnosis. A midlife career switch. Or maybe it crept in slowly, with the quiet dread of a life that just didn't fit anymore. It doesn't matter how it comes. What matters is what you *do* with it. Stoics believe that while we can't control what happens around us (other people's actions, weather, traffic, illness), we can control our responses, thoughts, and attitudes. Peace comes from focusing inward, not outward. Do you run from the fire? Or do you *rise* from it?

That's the lesson: Resilience doesn't show up in good times. It reveals itself in the wreckage. And if you're reading this thinking, *I'm still in the middle of the fire,* hang on. The wings come later. Tell the story that nearly broke you. Own the scar. And then show us how you turned it into something fierce, something strong, something *beautiful*. Because the world needs more phoenixes.

Week 18

Caring changes everything.

"Lean on Me"

—Bill Withers

Life Lesson

When I graduated with my master's degree at fifty-nine years old, our CFO took me to lunch to celebrate. Midway through the meal, he asked me a question I wasn't expecting. "If you had to write down everything you learned in grad school on the inside of a matchbook, what would it say?" I thought about it for a long time. I considered the frameworks, the research, the leadership theories, the models. But one word kept rising above the rest. "Caring," I said. He chuckled, almost dismissively. But I leaned in. "Hold on," I said. "Let me give you an example."

"Bob, let's say we allowed you to hire your recently graduated, unemployed daughter as your assistant. What would you do to make her successful?" Without hesitation, he replied, "I'd give her a strong onboarding plan. I'd connect her with the right people. I'd coach her, support her, open doors for her."

"Of course you would," I said. "Now, let me ask you about the accounting assistant who sits three cubicles down from you. She's worked for you for three years. Do you even know her last name? Do you know where she lives, what her goals are, or what's weighing on her right now?" He said nothing. "The difference between those two people is not competency or potential. It's how much you care. I'm not suggesting you care for her the same way you care for your daughter. But between *doing everything* for someone and *doing nothing* for someone, there's a massive gap."

I paused. "What if tomorrow morning you stopped by her desk and said, 'Debbie, you've worked for me for three years, and I owe you an apology. I haven't taken the time to really get to know you, and that's on me. I want to understand what you enjoy about your work, what frustrates you, and how I can better support you.'" Then I asked him, "What do you think her productivity would look like for the rest of the day?"

He sat back. He nodded slowly. "I get it," he said, "for the first time."

I'm not the first person to land on this truth. Scripture reminds us that among "faith, hope and love ... the greatest of these is love" (1

Corinthians 13:13). Maslow named love and belonging as necessary human needs.[9] John Maxwell said leaders should serve others and add value to their lives.[10] Jim Collins, in *Good to Great*, showed that greatness grows from discipline and intentional care.[11] Simon Sinek urged us to *Start with Why* because leading with purpose means leading with heart.[12] And Heather Younger wrote *The Art of Caring Leadership* as a guide to lifting others by leading with compassion.[13]

So why don't we hear this more often? We don't hear it because the *whats* of leading are almost obvious and are easy to understand, but the *hows are* hard. Doing the job, executing each of the activities of leadership, is the hard part.

Caring means listening without rushing. It means checking in without an agenda. It means giving help quietly, without the need for praise or attention. Caring isn't performative. If you do it just to be noticed, it rings hollow. People often want to talk about *psychological safety* (PS) in teams and workplaces. But PS isn't step one. It's the outcome. It's what happens *after* you've earned trust. Caring builds trust. Trust builds PS. PS creates connection. And connection is the foundation of everything meaningful, in leadership, in teams, and in life.

So maybe you won't need to know every leadership theory I studied. Maybe you won't need the acronyms or models. But if you want to lead well, and live well, start here: Care. It will change how you lead, how others feel when you leave the room, the legacy you will leave with people, and it might just change everything.

Week 19

Passionate people can learn anything.

"You Raise Me Up"
—Josh Groban

Life Lesson

Marcus Buckingham wrote in *Love + Work* that people should seek out work that feeds their red thread, what they are good at, and what they like.[14] We are generally passionate about something, even if we have trouble sorting it out at eighteen years old when the world wants you to make the life decisions that alter the course of your entire existence. I didn't discover mine, as you know by now, until I was fifty-nine years old.

There was one thing that fascinated me early on. My first father-in-law made a great impression on me. He -was a solid man, God driven, faithful, and deeply heartbroken when one of his kids would make a dumb move and get in legal trouble. His mother, Bam we called her, played guitar and sang Bible songs mostly. Dan played, too, and had an old original Gibson Hummingbird big box guitar. It had heavier-gauge strings, so if you started out to learn guitar on that thing, your fingers would go numb and sting. But I wanted to learn to play.

I moved to Hobbs, New Mexico, with my wife and infant son in 1978. I had a summer job there, and we could live with my parents rent-free. My son Josh spent one night sleeping in an open drawer as we had no crib. We never had a real honeymoon, so we stole away to El Paso for the Fourth of July weekend, and as I write this, it was forty-seven years ago this weekend. We walked over to Mexico, and I bought a guitar for twenty dollars. The neck was not reinforced, and the strings were old and hard to fret. Not knowing any better, when I got back to Hobbs on the Fourth, I went to the music store, and though closed, the owner was inside, and he sold me a book that had a few easy songs and pictures showing how to hold your hands to fret chords. For days, which morphed into a habit of years to come, I would hide away in the back of the house and learn the chords. I had no known music talent. Most people who begin learning acoustic guitar quit the first week because the steel strings are so painful to fret. Passion and pure desire to learn make the difference.

My fingers would almost bleed and were numb and sore for days at a time. "Longfellow's Serenade" was a song by Neil Diamond that you could play with just two or three chords. I learned to play that song with long pauses between the chord changes as I had to watch where I placed my fingers each time. So, from that humble beginning of a cheap Mexican guitar, I became a professional, self-taught musician overnight. Yep, it took only twenty years.

I was passionate about playing. The Church of Christ where my wife's family attended had no musical instruments. All singing was a capella. As a result, my boys and I learned to sing harmony without the aid of an instrument to find the notes. Singing came easier to me than playing, and for years I could not play an F chord—greatly limiting what songs I could play. This was before I discovered transposition and capos. They were game changers. There is something about my hands that do not allow me to play bar chords—also limiting. I found ways around it, even faking some of the chords in a way that no one would ever know—except those who knew.

Some years ago, a music patron came up during a show to say how much she enjoyed the show. I thanked her and told her how much that meant to me. I asked her what she liked most about the show. She said, "The song set." Looking at her, she was not far off my age. I play a lot of soft rock from the 1980s and stay in the James Taylor, Jackson Browne, Elton John, George Strait, and Billy Joel corner of the jukebox. I get a little wild with some Coldplay and Counting Crows. She didn't say she loved my silky voice or the picking and strumming. Nope. It was the song set. And you know what, I'm okay with that.

Passionate people can learn anything. Hire them. Now, after forty-seven years of playing, on being asked what I charge, I ask, "How far do I have to haul my equipment?" The farther it is, the more I charge. A few years back, I played forty-five shows in one year. During COVID, I played twenty-six shows from my dock for a hundred homes within earshot to entertain the locked-down neighbors. I played free, but the neighbors insisted on tipping, so I set it up where tips went to the Food Bank, and we fed a meal to eighteen thousand out-of-work people. The news ran a story on a slow news day. The playing benefited us all.

If I can entertain people and hold them all night at a wine bar or brewery, then I have done my job well. I am passionate about all of it—especially the curated song set. And passionate people are powerful.

Week 20

You can do hard things.

"I Will Survive"

—Gloria Gaynor

Life Lesson

I was afraid. When I got the call that my girlfriend was pregnant, my whole life plan suddenly shattered. Everything I thought I knew about my future cracked under the weight of reality. When the oil and gas industry collapsed in the mid-1980s and I found myself shipped off to Alaska to a field job above the Arctic Circle, I was frozen in more ways than one. That wasn't adventure. That was survival. Then, just weeks into our new life in the vast, isolated wild of Alaska, our six-month-old son developed a hernia. Terrified, we wondered what kind of witch doctor might be waiting in Anchorage. Turns out, the head of pediatric surgery at Cedars-Sinai Hospital in Los Angeles had just moved to Anchorage, so we were all good.

In the middle of changing careers, finally, to one I liked and suited me, my first wife fell into a deep, suffocating depression. I became the only fully functioning parent of two young boys, and I was overwhelmed. The weight of being "the rock" was crushing. It was not and never was her fault. But our lives had to be managed. She still is a sweet lady regardless of our struggles. I had become accustomed to tragedy and hopelessness. They are familiar foes. Seeing her suffer for no apparent reason was hard. Logic has no place in depression. When I took the role of lobbyist, I was gone a week at a time, once or twice each month. It hurt leaving her, and the potential for this leading to a different and more lucrative career was the dream I was clinging to. Maybe we could move back to the South somewhere. Maybe it was separation from her parents that led her to this depression, and maybe I could fix that. It was mental cruelty to watch her fight the demons no one else could see. After eight more years of her condition getting progressively worse, the hopelessness was insurmountable.

Divorce did not show up in my family anywhere. My backpack was heavy. I couldn't escape it. Having to tell my kids that their mom and I were getting a divorce was one of the hardest moments of my life. We were headed into Thanksgiving, and the boys were going to Oklahoma to be with their maternal grandparents. Keaton, at nine years old, didn't completely understand, but when I married Reneé pretty quickly and he got two built-in playmates who served as distractions, well, that made everything better. Josh, at nearly seventeen years old, was a harder sell. Even though he had watched his mother decline in functionality with the weight of depression, there was a very strong mother-son bond—as there should be. The struggle was real. I felt sorry for him for what I was doing.

There was no blueprint for divorce and separation. It was uncharted territory, and with a partially functioning wife and children from adolescence to elementary school, it added to the "challenge, change, and complexity" of my life, to use Dr. Taryn Marie's words.[15] It drained me. Emptied me. Left me hollow. It doesn't matter who's at fault—grief carves its initials on your soul either way.

Losing both of my parents in 2022 was devastating. My mom had been in poor health, so losing her, while tragic, was expected. Though no consolation for losing your life mate of sixty-six years, my dad was now free to re-engage his life. And he died trying, literally.

He was my best friend and trusted advisor. We loved football in the fall and golf in the spring. He loved to cook and was a great teacher of culinary arts. Losing him left a huge hole that I have never found a way to fill.

I was the executor of my dad's estate, a title that sounds important and mostly means you handle everyone's heartbreak while burying your own. Selling the house and the cars, managing the transfer of assets, and processing my own grief left a scar. And somewhere in there, I realized I had stopped breathing freely for two years.

Life comes with hard times. I felt like I had more than my share. Sometimes I reread Dr. Taryn Marie's book on resilience just to re-center and re-remember those times as constructive instead of destructive. Most people never face even one of these situations in a lifetime. I've faced more than I ever wanted and lived to tell it. I didn't learn these lessons in a classroom. Life beat them into me. And here's the truth that no textbook teaches: You can do hard things. Even the ones that feel impossible.

Some people are born bold. Confident. Maybe even cocky. That kind of untested swagger probably helps them sleep better at night. But

I wasn't wired that way. My dad, smart, tough, driven, just wanted his kids to have more than he did. But his high expectations sometimes left us feeling like we were never quite enough. So, confidence didn't come naturally to me. It came kicking and screaming, forged in fire. Eleanor Roosevelt said, "You gain strength, courage, and confidence by every experience in which you really stop to look fear in the face." She was right. People say, "If you're going through hell, keep going." It's more than a cliché. If you're truly *going through* something, that means there's an "after" waiting on the other side. Don't ever mistake confidence for having it all figured out. Real confidence is still scary. It's stitched together from the wreckage of things we swore we couldn't survive.

Think back on your own life. What have you made it through? If you're like me, the hardest stuff, the real heartbreaks, left a mark. They're unforgettable. And that's the point. Because growth screams in chaos.

Now here I sit in a serene coffee shop on Main Street in Bozeman, Montana. It is Sunday morning. Daybreak. A cold June rain taps the windows. The light poles shine like they're wrapped in glass. And peace hangs in the air like a hymn. The peace I feel now is the win. The hard things didn't break me. I got a chance to *feel* again. I take mental inventory of all the things I thought would break me. And I realize, I made it through. Everything will be okay. It may not feel like it in the moment. But I promise you this ...

You can do hard things.

Week 21

Be optimistic.

"Here Comes the Sun"

—The Beatles

Life Lesson

My wife continually sees me as a glass-half-empty person. It may be that I spend so much of my professional life elevating people and solving people problems that I am tired of people by the time I get home. Maybe at sixty-seven, I'm just male, pale, and stale. It also is a sign that I absorbed a bit of my dad's personality too. Though I don't think I am that insecure. I think it was his meager beginnings and rising up from a form of involuntary, family-forced servitude in a sharecropper life that shaped him. I want to be remembered as a positive person. I don't think my wife gets to see me in my element listening to difficult problems at work and successfully turning them around. We could take a lesson from her. She never complains about anything.

I read a lot. Mostly about people. Mostly about people at work. I recently came across several thought pieces that add up for me around attitude. We dismissed positive mental attitude (PMA) in the '70s as faddish. We heard Zig Ziglar say it in his blockbuster book *See You at the Top* and in motivational talks for decades: "Your attitude, not your aptitude, will determine your altitude."[16] Then in the book *Breaking the Age Code*, Becca Levy's studies on aging say that those with an optimistic view live longer.[17] We hear entrepreneurs like Jess Ekstrom say every successful venture started with someone's solid belief in their own success.[18]

The main lesson from the movie *The Secret* by Rhonda Byrne is the power of the "law of attraction," which suggests that thoughts and feelings can directly influence external reality.[19] By focusing on positive thoughts and visualizing desired outcomes, the movie implies that individuals can manifest their goals and dreams. This is commonly referred to as "the universe." Some refer to "the universe" as a more abstract, benevolent force that orchestrates events for us, and we are just along for the ride. Some see "signs" or "messages" from the universe in coincidences or seemingly random events, suggesting that these events are not random but part of a larger plan. It is their religion of sorts.

With optimism in our lives, maybe the subconscious mind is more influential and powerful, and our success is manifested more than we know. We are our worst critics—at least those who have some humility. But we *can* be our biggest fan. Simon Sinek has a podcast called *A Bit of Optimism*.[20] Sinek began the podcast during COVID as a source of hope. Adam Grant interviewed Susan David on overcoming toxic positivity, and Adam shared, "Optimism is born of a willingness to show up to the reality. It is born of a belief that the future can be better, and optimism is also born of a willingness to put in the work."[21] So measured positivity as optimism can be a good friend, propel success, and cause you to live better and longer. There is something here.

I'm optimistic. Some believe that there are powers in the universe or that "the universe" is communicating with them on the daily. I'm not going to talk much about religion here, but I have come to know some things. There are many people more convicted than me about their religious beliefs. I have a tough time believing that there is no accommodation for those who think differently than me about the afterlife. And if God wanted Christians to be more convicted about their afterlife beliefs, wouldn't he, "or she," have been more explicit in the book of Revelation about what heaven is like and how we get there? Jews, Muslims, and Christians all share the Old Testament. After that it gets wonky. We talk about what happens with our spirit when we die, but we never talk about our spirit arriving from somewhere when we are born. Is it recycled? Does it get created? If so, from where? And how does it enter us?

So don't waste your time criticizing other belief systems. Be optimistic that there is an answer for everyone. Have confidence, be positive, and be optimistic with others. They will find their way out of difficulty. Whether prayer is communicating with a deity or if it is simply thinking deeply in a quiet space and channeling goodness, like *The Secret*, don't discount it. There is evidence that there is power in optimistic thought.

Week 22

Have friends across multiple generations.

"We Are Family"
—Sister Sledge

Life Lesson

I was born in and lived in Shreveport, Louisiana, until I was nine years old. The crazy 1960s. My life was a picture out of a *Leave it to Beaver* episode. We played outside until the streetlights came on. We climbed trees, went to Cub Scouts, camped on family vacations, and rode in cars without seat belts. We were warned about the evils of drugs and watched the Vietnam War on TV every night—tape-delayed and still jarring.

My dad was a petroleum engineer, and the pipeline work often took him far from home. Then he started working on his master's degree at Louisiana Tech in Ruston, over an hour away, spending weekends in class. We only had one car, so his absence became even more noticeable. During those years, I didn't see him much at all.

Thankfully, our neighbors stepped in. The Deatons lived next door on one side, and the Simmons family lived on the other side.

Mr. Simmons noticed I didn't yet know how to ride a bike. One day, he walked me to the sidewalk, jogged alongside, let go without telling me—and just like that, I was riding. Mrs. Simmons, a former army nurse, had a knack for teaching. She realized I didn't know how to tie my shoes and taught me a shortcut in ten minutes flat. Our families camped in Arkansas together, shared countless backyard cookouts, and in many ways, they became second and third parents to me.

Eventually, life took us all in different directions. The Deatons moved to the country, the Simmonses to Norway, and we moved to Lafayette when my dad graduated. Over the next twenty years, we rarely saw each other.

Then, in one of those small miracles of timing, the Simmonses moved to Spring, Texas—not far from me. By then my parents had lived all over the world—Canada, Egypt, Russia—but I reconnected with the people who had once taught me to ride a bike and tie my shoes.

After Mrs. Simmons passed away, I visited Mr. Simmons often. He told me oil field stories from his years in Norway, and we laughed about how I used to wake him from his Sunday nap to ask if his daughter,

Carrie, could come out and play. I was honored to serve as a pallbearer at his funeral years later.

It's funny how relationships shift over time. As a child, Mr. Simmons was a father figure. Later, he was a friend from my dad's generation. Today, I have friends who are younger than my oldest son and friends who are my age—or older.

Søren Kierkegaard once said that life is lived forward and understood backward. Looking back, I realize that had my dad not been away so often, I might not have formed such a deep connection with our neighbors. Those friendships lasted decades even with long periods of absence without seeing each other.

As an adult, I've been a "stand-in dad" at high school father-daughter events for friends of my kids who didn't have a dad in their lives. These relationships never really die. Those kids remember, and you remember how it made you feel to make them feel included.

Having friends of different ages not only enriches our lives with unique perspectives, but it also keeps us more open, more accepting, and more complete. In our relationships, diversity in age, like diversity in background, makes us better people—widening the range of what we understand, value, and cherish.

Week 23

Where there is no struggle, there is much less learning.

"The Climb"
—*Miley Cyrus*

Life Lesson

"You should probably wear gloves," he said, "because if I miss and hit your hand, at least all the pieces will be in one place."

It was about 105 degrees. Late August 1977 in western Kansas, near Ness City. My last day on my first industrial summer job before heading back to college. I was a roustabout.

A roustabout is basically a lackey with a pulse—an extra pair of hands to hold, carry, fetch, and to kick piles of metal to check for snakes. We crawled into tight spaces, grabbed things too hot to touch, and did whatever no one else wanted to do. I've never been to jail, but I imagine this was close to "hard labor." By eight a.m., just ninety minutes into the workday, the heat, wheat stubble, and dry wind made the day feel miserable—whether you were working or not.

We pulled up to a pump jack, one of those rocking horse-looking contraptions, about ten to fifteen feet tall, that pulls oil up from a deep well when it won't flow on its own. The supervisor told me we had to adjust the wrist pins, which meant shortening or lengthening the pump's stroke. What he didn't tell me—until we were standing there—was that this involved pounding out a three-inch diameter steel pin with a sixteen-pound sledgehammer. And someone had to hold a two-inch steel pipe over the pin while the other swung for the fences, hoping he didn't miss.

Guess who got the "holding" job.

Everything was scorching from the Kansas sun—tools, pipe, even the air felt like it could burn you. That's when he made his glove suggestion—half safety tip, half gallows humor.

I didn't say no. I needed that job next summer, and I needed his recommendation to get it. So, I closed my eyes, gripped that pipe as steadily as I could, and waited for him to swing. A dozen hits later, the pin came free—and somehow, my hands were still intact. He never missed.

Those were different times. Safety protocols existed mostly as suggestions. Today it would never happen. I could call it a lesson in trust. Or a rite of passage. But honestly, it was just one chapter in a summer that saw me get an almost heart-stopping electric jolt, abandon my law school dreams, marry my pregnant girlfriend, figure out how to get back to college, change my major, and work harder than I ever worked in my life.

I arrived in Kansas soft-handed and naive, bouncing along on the American Dream. I left ninety days later, married, wiser, and older in ways that had nothing to do with birthdays—though with plenty of rough roads still ahead. That day was trial by fire, sink or swim, under the gun, through the wringer, and on the hot seat all rolled into one.

It lasted maybe thirty minutes, and almost fifty years later, the memory is still vivid. After having managed safety for a few companies, been in confined spaces, climbed way higher than I was comfortable, and stood in the living rooms of widows and orphans who lost their loved one doing their job, I am passionate about being safe. Today, I'd tell Jerry, "That's not safe and not worth the risk. Let's think of a better way."

What about you? What's one of your most resilient moments, the one that changed you to the core? The one you prayed would pass, cried through, or wondered if it was worth it?

If you came out the other side, I can tell you—it was worth it. We have a saying in human resources when managers try something like firing someone for the first time: "But did you die?" It doesn't work for my wife. As a nurse supervisor, maybe *she* didn't die, but if she doesn't do her job well every minute of every day, someone *might* die.

Every life experience is additive. "It all adds up!" Thank you, Wendell Schuman, my friend, for that gem. We are the sum of our experience. The bad ones are the ones that stick with us longer. We are better for living through each of them. We appreciate it—but not until it's over.

Week 24

Followship is about relationships.

"With a Little Help from My Friends"

—Joe Cocker

Life Lesson

When I was still new to being a vice president of human resources, I went on my "press the flesh" tour of our locations at a new company. The company was the smallest of my career, and it was international to match my new master's degree endeavor—distance learning from Liverpool, England. One stop on the tour was in Lafayette, Louisiana, a small office with wholesome small-town people. They were friendly and seemed a little overdressed for our tank washing shop, and very proud of their work. A tank wash shop is where stainless steel chemical tanks are washed for re-use. They are usually rentals that are recycled for another renter.

The front of the building had a few offices, the back had a break/training room, and restrooms. They were the "one hole" kind. The coffee pot was clearly overworked, and the calcium in the water left it looking like it had survived a war. This was the oil field, and no one gave it a second thought.

Over the years, I learned that if you really want to understand a company's culture, talk to the administrative staff. They are the keepers of the truth. So I always made a point to bring in lunch and spend time with them.

That Friday, we were in the conference room, again—a surprisingly nice one for a tank wash shop. I shared that I'd spent half my elementary and junior high years not far from there and asked what was going on that weekend. It was Friday in the fall, and the whole town was buzzing about the "Friday night lights" of the high school football game.

One admin grinned and said, "Ginger usually wears her son's football jersey to work on game days. It's a big deal." I looked at Ginger. She was in a skirt and blouse—polished and definitely not Friday spirit wear. I asked, "Ginger, why no jersey today?" She looked down and mumbled, "Because you were coming to visit."

That one hit me.

I inquired further, "Wait—were you told not to wear it, or did you just decide?"

"No," she said, "Benny told us yesterday not to wear our normal Friday clothes because you were coming."

This was the first time I realized my job title could get in the way of connecting with people.

"Let's get one thing straight," I said. "I'm just another worker here, same payroll system, same benefits. I may have more people reporting to me, but that's not about power—it's about building relationships so we can do more good work together. I want to know what's working and what's not. No shiny-penny talk. Tell me the truth, and I'll do the same."

The conversation loosened up. They told me they normally wore jeans, boots, and "spirit wear" on Fridays. I apologized for them missing their day and made it clear, as long as it's tasteful, wear what makes you comfortable. Spirit days are only a season in your life. One day you will look back and forget the cost of raising kids and the frenetic pace of these days, and you will remember the good in each of these days. You will miss this. You will miss the excitement in the eyes of the youth.

I didn't get to meet the real Friday Ginger that day. She lost one of her ten Friday Spirit Days that year—because of me. It was a hard lesson I'll never forget. Titles can open doors, and they can also close hearts.

From that day forward, I knew my position could unintentionally create distance. John Maxwell calls "position" the first level of leadership—it doesn't make you a leader.[22] In fact, it might be the very thing that stands between you and truly knowing your people. So be the one who gets up to shake hands. Stand when your lunch guest arrives late to the table. When they have a name on their shirt and you don't, they are the most important person in the room. They are the ones who make your life possible. Salute them.

They are the important ones.

Week 25

Perform acts of kindness for those unable to reciprocate.

"Humble and Kind"
—*Tim McGraw*

Life Lesson

I don't want to overstate this or make it into some martyrdom situation, but getting the girls as bonus daughters was a gift when I married Reneé. And the best way to pay her back, extending the gratitude it deserves, would be in becoming their dad—a real, functioning, interested dad. At eight years old and before we were even married, Jordan would be sniffling in bed over some school thing where she was left out of a clique or someone cut in line ahead of her. You know, Earth-moving stuff of being eight. I would sit and listen and tell her that there would be lots of days like that in her life, but that she needed to know that love heals a lot of things. I would do my best Fred Rogers of Mr. Rogers fame. Love from her mom and from me would always be her haven—a place where she could tell us all her fears and know that we would always be here for her. I would get these sweet, freshly brushed teeth kisses on the cheek, and off to sleep she would go. That would be and has always been my thank-you to Reneé. But it is my greatest gift to myself. At almost forty years old, that little girl is still in there at times, but what she doesn't know is that missing her by a ferry ride and a couple of hours as I blew through Seattle last weekend was *my* loss. I am the one with the gratitude for her gift of trust and love for me.

Most people you meet today are walking around with something heavy, not their huge bag of laundry to drop at the cleaners, or their hand-carried, thousand-pound super cooler of mocktail mixers, or the giant ugly floor vase they got at the white elephant holiday party last year. No, I'm talking about the invisible backpack they carry around every single day. That load people carry is filled with life's greatest burdens: family health, finances, loneliness. You know, the same things you are inventorying right now in your head. Some of us are barely holding it together. Some don't even realize how heavy it's gotten. And that's why even the smallest act of kindness hits like a lightning bolt. When someone, anyone, sees you, *really sees you* and does something unexpectedly kind, it feels like the universe just gave you a little wink. It's like coming home and discovering a surprise Amazon package you forgot you ordered—and better, because this one landed right on your soul. Gratitude or giving back is the secret to healing life's difficulties. Let me give you a few examples that stuck with me.

Buying Girl Scout Cookies is a good thing. It may be the slightest bit annoying because you've already bought a box or three from your niece, from your boss's daughter, and from the random knock on the door with an irresistible smile, and you still aren't done. The next trip to the grocery store, and there they are again, like a fortress around the entrance of the store with overachieving mothers correcting the delivery of the kid's pitch in real time. I finally had to make a little game out of it. Once I had my winter store of the little morsels, I began to do something different with each buying opportunity. I now buy a box from the snaggletoothed little girl leaning on the bin of watermelons as she stares at her feet while asking, "Sir, would you like to buy some Girl Scout Cookies?" I tell her, "I'll take one box. And please give this delicious box of cookies to the next person who looks like they need a little joy or maybe just can't afford it right now." That tiny box will more than brighten someone else's day, someone not expecting a gift, and it will give the little girl a story to tell and the recipient a moment of grace. And me? Well, I get to skip the calories and still feel full.

Another example: opening a door. Yep, it can be that simple. I hold doors open for everyone. It isn't just a Southern thing (though I was raised by a blue-collar debutante, so it's practically genetic for me). It is a basic, beautiful act of decency. And at that moment, holding the door for a tired parent, a struggling elder, or a stranger who didn't see it coming, it just *feels good.*

I once helped load a case of water into someone's trunk. An older lady in the parking lot, clearly with mobility issues, needed help getting a flat of water from her cart to her trunk. That took maybe twelve seconds of my day. And I walked away with a lifted heart. Maybe helping that lady with the water was the best thing that happened to her all day. Maybe it was the only kind thing. Either way, I felt better, and that's the secret—the gift. When you do good, *you* feel good. Just like paying for the coffee for the person behind you in the drive-through line. Classic. Simple. Magic.

My friend, Jared Hamilton, another CPO (chief people officer), did an informal study in his company comparing those who participated in their gratitude/shout-out program to those who did not participate. Those who showed gratitude had a significantly higher engagement score, meaning they cared more about the company, its future, and their own contribution than those who did not express gratitude. So empirically, it is true. Gratitude for the win!

Nowadays, we all need new and more ways to feel good about ourselves, about life, and about faith in humanity. So today, look around. Opportunities to be kind are everywhere: Text a friend you haven't spoken to in months. Leave a little extra tip for the breakfast server who's already refilled your coffee four times. You know they have the worst shifts and the smallest checks of the day. Send flowers for no reason. No reason is the best reason. Write a thank-you note to someone who isn't expecting it. Call your mom or your dad. Or the person who's shown up like one. Do not do it because you have to do it. Do it because you can. Because kindness might just be the one thing you give away that comes back tenfold.

But here's a pro tip: Don't wait for applause. If you expect someone to acknowledge your good deed, you might end up disappointed. And that robs you of the self-lifting power of the act. When someone *does* thank you, soak it in. That feeling? That's your invisible backpack getting a little lighter. And please resist the urge to tell the world. I know, I know ... it feels important to share. And we live in an age where "virtue signaling" is a full-time job. Sometimes the kindest act that gives *you* the most value is the one you keep to yourself. Let it live quietly in your chest, warming you when you need it most. *You know you did good. That's enough.* As my friend Darryl Preen wisely says, "Better is better." Even in small doses.

He's right. Kindness is a medicine, free to give and to feel it come back—and impossible to overdose on. It is best taken twice daily with food. For me, everything is better with food. You're not going to save the world in a day, but string enough of these little acts of kindness together over time, and you can create a culture of it in your life. It could become part of your brand. "They" will say kind things about you when you leave the room. It can become your new legacy. You can make someone's world a little better in a moment.

And maybe you make *your* own world a bit better in the process too.

Week 26

Others see more in you than you do.

"I Believe in You"
—Don Williams

Life Lesson

I sometimes wonder out loud if every teenager feels invisible and unheard. We moved a lot when I was young. By the time I was fourteen, I'd lived in three different places, never long enough to build lasting friendships. I landed in Oklahoma, a place behind the times but a leap ahead of Louisiana. Popular music would not be heard on the Oklahoma City radio stations until months later than the rest of the country. That's how everything felt: Late. Including me.

Looking back, I think I was depressed when we moved to Oklahoma. I was withdrawn, quiet, forgotten, and alone. My grades started to slip. By the time I entered tenth grade at Putnam City High School, my GPA was just a notch above 2.0. I wasn't hanging out with kids who cared. These weren't driven honor roll kids. Not bad kids, just not the ones to spur me to academic greatness. I got comfortable with less focus on school. I was bouncing along, month by month.

And then, out of nowhere, I got called to the counselor's office. Ms. Nona Cowan, who never married and drove a canary-yellow VW Beetle, sat me down and told me I'd been awarded the Student of Today award by the American Legion. I remember thinking, *What organization goes out of its way to honor an invisible, below-average, skinny, pale, rudderless kid with bad hair?* When the day of the award ceremony came, I got dressed up in a nice collared shirt and new pants, and we headed to the American legion building. My parents came to the ceremony, likely equally in amazement. I stood there for pictures, holding a framed certificate, wondering what on earth they saw in me. A few weeks passed. I kept the framed certificate in a prominent place in my room at home. The award was for something specific, I guess. It said something about me, but I couldn't quite put my finger on it.

A few weeks went by. Again, I was summoned to Ms. Cowan's office. She told me she was placing me in Honors English for my junior year. I broke into a sweat. I don't remember asking why. The last formal English class I was in, I got a D after one of the nine-week periods and had to have a form signed by my parents. I'm sure that was a proud dad moment—for the guy who insisted on good grades. This could not possibly end well.

That fall, I walked into a room full of the "cool kids," not the party cool—the smart cool. They welcomed me. The conversation wasn't about who skipped class or how little you studied. It was about flash cards, test prep, and acing the next quiz. Suddenly, studying was cool, and I needed to be included. So, to fit in, I strapped in. I read, I highlighted, I took notes and rewrote them for the pure learning impact.

The pure math said it would take straight A's for the rest of my high school days to bring the two-point-nothing GPA to the 3.5 needed to be an honor graduate. It became almost an obsession.

The next year, I took a grammar and composition class, where I discovered something unexpected: I was pretty good at writing. Our teacher required us to enter a writing contest as part of our final grade. I entered the Ability Counts essay contest run by the Disabled American Veterans. The essay highlighted three people who excelled at their chosen profession because of their resilience. It was several pages long. The center thought was a cottonwood tree—a true story. Lightning had struck it, and new growth was coming out of the very place that was burned and damaged. I connected that thought to those who had persevered through their disabilities to excel, not in spite of but, in some ways, because of their limitations. I won first place in the State of Oklahoma. Then fifth in the nation. I got a two-year paid scholarship to a state school. I flew on a plane for the first time. It was a trip to Washington, DC, to accept the fifth-place award. We stayed in a fancy hotel where the doors opened to a hallway on the inside of the building instead of the parking lot balcony. The air conditioner was nowhere to be found; it wasn't some cream-colored unit with a trap door on top hiding the "cooler" and "hotter" controls. As part of the program there was a super fancy dinner, a tour of the monuments at night, and in a special ceremony, the top five winners got to lay a wreath at the Tomb of the Unknown Soldier. Harold Russell, who had lost his hands in World War II and then won an Academy Award for his role in the 1946 movie *The Best Years of Our Lives*, presented me with my award.

What I didn't know at the time was that scholarship was the only way I could have managed to go to college after getting married at nineteen to a pregnant wife, both of us fighting for a future with blood, sweat, and literal tears. And yet all of it, *all of it*, traces back to a moment in Ms. Cowan's office. A moment of faith, asking and listening to understand me. How did she know how I would react to a single small award and an unwelcomed placement in Honors English? I went on to be VP of the senior class, attended Boys' State (a week-long civics camp that simulates the state government process), and made that 3.5 GPA in my last semester. Her intuition changed everything.

I couldn't thank Ms. Cowan in the way that she deserved. I decided to thank her in the way that she would have preferred by becoming all that she would have wanted me to be. As proud of me as I knew she was when I won the writing contest, I knew I could do something that would honor her. I believe her secret was in the way she made you feel in her presence. She listened to you, the leaning-in kind of listening. Not only did you feel heard, but you felt validated. Listening is a keystone of my leadership model, and now I can point to the story I have about her as a premier example.

I never got to say thank you. When the internet became powerful enough, I set about finding her. I did. It was her obituary from just ten months earlier. I was grateful that I found her, and I was heartbroken that I could not remind her of the greatest gift I ever received. Because she saw me, I started seeing myself. Some people come into our lives like flashbulbs—bright, brief, unforgettable. They don't just give you advice; they listen. They give you *belief*. Sometimes, that's all a person needs.

Week 27

Live in every dusty corner of your life.

"Life's a Dance"

—John Michael Montgomery

Life Lesson

About fifteen years ago, my wife and I traveled to Todos Santos, Mexico, about an hour north of Cabo San Lucas on the Baja California peninsula. It is a sleepy little Mexican village on the Pacific side of Baja. On the way there, we stopped at a dusty roadside cantina called Art and Beer. It is owned by an artist and his wife, who have little more than a large palapa under which is a huge round bar where he makes his twenty-plus ingredient Bloody Marys. They also own a school bus, which we assume does not run, and we think they live in it. It is worth the stop.

In Todos Santos, there is an inn called Hotel California. The Eagles deny any connection, but all of the pieces fit as I did a photo montage of the dark desert highway leading to the inn, the mission next door, the dark open-air corridors, etc. Across the street is the obligatory T-shirt shop for Hotel California merchandise, making the attraction legit. Ironically, this Mexican inn was founded in 1947 by Mr. Wong, a Chinese immigrant. In 2001, John and Debbie Stewart took over. On our first visit, we spent a long time with Debbie and John. They are Canadians, and Debbie was the mastermind of a fantastic renovation. Her freshly squeezed orange juice mimosas are worth the trip. During the conversation, Debbie heard my wife talk about the rooms in our house we just didn't use, the formal living room and the breakfast area. She cautioned Reneé to make every room livable in the house. Upon our return home, Reneé converted the breakfast area into a sitting room off the kitchen and hung a chandelier. She converted the formal living/dining room with a large, casual, eight-person conversational wooden dining table and wrought iron accented chairs. We often quote Debbie about not waiting to enjoy our house, gathering the things we were waiting to buy in retirement, and visiting the places we want to see while we are young enough to enjoy them. In another piece of dark irony, when we returned to Hotel California a few years later, John had died. It was almost poetic that Debbie insisted we live in every dusty corner of our lives while we could and then lost John shortly after. I know that for John it was never about the size of his inn; it was about the fact that every bit of it was lived in. Just as Debbie was able to squeeze every drop of juice from the orange for her mimosas, they were able to squeeze every drop of life from what they had.

In a similar fashion, my friend Darryl has a hashtag "75" board, meaning a plan to accomplish all of his life goals, personal and professional, by the time he is seventy-five years old. He even has a counter on his phone that tells him how many weeks he has left. He is aware of seizing every moment as it comes. I admire that about him. Squeeze that fruit!

Since we first talked to Debbie at the inn, and especially with Reneé's cancer journey, we have begun to travel to the places we were saving for retirement. I bought a Mini Cooper base model after one of my HR friends died at fifty-two years old, realizing that at my age I may reach a point overnight where I can't drive a fun car. At our new house of ten years, we don't have a formal dining room; we have one comfortable living area and several gathering areas for conversation, and we live on a small lake in the suburbs. We see our kids around the country as often as possible, as we do the math on how many visits we have left to see them.

I have a friend who with his wife eats every meal with silverware. Not stainless-steel tableware. Silver. Silver spoons, silver knives, silver forks. Their grandma's silver gets used every single day in their house. He said, "Know that if you come over to my house to eat a peanut butter sandwich, it will be spread with a silver knife. When it was handed down to us, I made it clear that I wasn't going to store it for thirty years and then hand it to my daughter to worry about."

I have bourbon glasses I've collected from famous distilleries around the country and the world. I have some from the Kentucky Derby. I have some that roll around with a glass ball on the bottom. I drink from them all!

I have a few souvenir whiskeys that look good on the shelf. It is just a matter of time before they are consumed in celebration of some odd-numbered Tuesday—I celebrate everything.

We sat in the two stadium seats that I'd bought when they dismantled the Astrodome in 2013. I gave them to my parents as a gift, since they were big Astros fans. When they passed away in 2022, I brought the seats to my house. They are authentic, certified sports memorabilia and collectors' items, but they are cool chairs too. When the Astrodome opened in 1965, it was a one-of-a-kind indoor sports venue. People still refer to it as the Eighth Wonder of the World. The Astrodome was such a big part of my history with my mom. She loved the Astros games, especially when she could go with my two boys. It's about living in *every dusty corner*!

Vivian Greene, a romance novelist, said, "Life isn't about waiting for the storm to pass; it's about learning to dance in the rain." When you get older, it feels like there are more cloudy and rainy days. Health and financial struggles occur, and friends pass away with more frequency. Those are rainy days. Accepting those challenges and learning to live within and around them is sage advice. I guess we are just back to seizing the day. Henry David Thoreau said, "Fools stand on their island of opportunities and look toward another land. There is no other land; there is no other life."

Live in every room in your house and in your life.

SOUND
LIKE
WEATHER

Part II – Relational Wisdom

The Art of Leading Through Connection

No leader thrives alone. Influence is born through connection—through empathy, listening, and the grace to let others be seen and heard. Relational wisdom is about learning the language of others, not expecting them to learn ours.

The following reflections explore the subtle art of leading through relationships: the power of generosity, the patience of listening, and the humility to value followship as much as leadership. They challenge us to see the humanity in those around us—to love people and use things, not the other way around.

Our friendships, our families, our teams—they all hold mirrors up to the kind of leader we are becoming. The question isn't how many people follow you; it's how many people you lift along the way.

Week 28

Listen generously until the other person feels heard.

"Listen to the Music"
—*The Doobie Brothers*

Life Lesson

When I *preach* leadership, I am passionate, whether at home or at work. This week's lesson shows that leadership starts with the heart.

That's where *generous listening* comes in.

Generous listening isn't just letting someone talk while you politely nod. It's giving your full attention—leaning in, holding eye contact, staying present. It's something the other person should *feel*, not just see. And it's surprisingly easy to mess up. Glancing at your watch, answering a text, or scanning the room like a squirrel just darted past? That's a fast track to making someone feel unimportant.

There was a gruff old drilling superintendent from my days in Alaska who was, by design, intimidating. He was not classically trained. He had no engineering degree, and he had to interpret what an engineer was saying, judge it from an operational perspective, and either implement the recommendation, augment the recommendation, or, as happened most often, tell the engineer to "pound sand!"

When I was leaving the engineering group to begin my lobbying career, I went to his office to thank him for being patient with me as I learned what I needed to know to be a better engineer (I was never going to be a good one). Seeing my effort and diligence, he said to me, "Keep doing what you are doing. You are going to do great things." I never knew he felt that way.

Generous listening means asking clarifying questions, repeating back what you think you heard, and making sure they know you understand their point—especially when it matters to them. When people can consistently count on us to really listen, we start building trust.

Marcus Buckingham puts it well in *Love + Work* that trust—not talent—is the greatest asset of any organization.[23] Without it, even the best teams will never reach their full potential.

Because human resources people live in a confidential bubble, we don't talk about specifics of what is shared in my office. I have heard women say they were being abused and thanked me for listening and pointing them to resources. I have had men tell me their wife was raped the night before. Those words still rock me when I think about it. In that moment, people just need a safe place to emote and be heard. We in HR are not equipped and should not attempt to be counselors or therapists. We are to listen and point them to help. It takes an extra gene to be able to hear these tragedies and finish your mundane paper-pushing part of the job.

But here's the catch: The *what* is always easier than the *how*. Truly listening—without planning your rebuttal or waiting for your chance to "one-up" their story—is hard. Most of us carry around what I call an "emotional bucket" that is running low. Maslow was right: Significance, belonging, and attention are critical human needs. We're all just hoping someone will help fill our bucket a little.

So, what does generous listening actually look like? I work hard at this in my job. Picture this: Someone sits down across from me to share a problem—sometimes trivial, but sometimes someone in their family is dying or threatening to hurt themselves. Within thirty seconds, I think I know the answer or at least some advice that will help immediately. I'm itching to jump in. But instead of waiting for a breath to bulldoze my way in, I forcibly stop myself to ensure I let them finish. Completely. Then I validate:

- "Wow, I can tell you're passionate about this."
- "That sounds like it's been weighing on you. Is there more you want me to know?"

Only after you're sure they've said all they need to say should you share your perspective—gently and with care. "I can see how that would be challenging for even the most experienced person. I've had a slightly different experience—would you like to hear it?"

Michael Bungay Stanier, in *The Coaching Habit*, says the key is to stay curious longer.[24] He's talking about coaching. The principle works everywhere—in the office, at the dinner table, in casual conversations with friends.

Generous listening is an act of patience. It's a choice to make *their* story more important than your reply. And in doing so, you're not just hearing their words, you're filling their bucket, strengthening trust, and leading from the heart.

It's not the grand speeches or impressive titles that people remember; it's how we make them feel. The building blocks of leadership in every area of life begin with genuine care for another human being's well-being. Once that's established, the next layer is respect. And the best way to show respect? Make sure a person feels seen and heard.

Week 29

You don't have to attend every argument you are invited to.

"Let It Go"

—Idina Menzel

Life Lesson

What I like most about maturing? Not much. It comes at the cost of getting older or paying the toll of consequences. Wisdom is built on a tall stack of failures, and if you're lucky, you learn something each time you fall. There was a time when I thought I was smarter than most people. I wasn't. And wow, that's a tall ladder to fall from. *For most of us*, failure, paired with a good dose of embarrassment or admonishment, is enough to set us straight. We see the warning signs next time and steer clear.

But then there are those who never seem fazed by negative feedback. They're not oblivious; they just can't bear being wrong. Look around; if you have no friends, you're not invited to gatherings, employees won't work for you, and no one asks your opinion, it's not bad luck. It's behavior.

It was in dealing with a true know-it-all that I finally let go of the idea that I could educate them. With some people, generous listening and relationship-building simply don't work. The truth gets tangled with imagination until, even to you, it sounds like the world is always on their side. That's when you start getting invitations—invites to arguments. That is their game.

One day, I was asked to pick up some "artesian" (are-TEEZE-shun) bread at a farm-to-market store. Not being a culinary scholar or a regular at farm-to-market stores, I searched high and low for artesian bread. Then I saw a hand-drawn sign for "artisan" (ARE-tiz-an) bread. Thinking I'd misheard the name, I bought the artisan bread for the dinner party.

Weeks later, my wife was at dinner with the same guy and decided to poke the bear. "So," she said, "the other day, you referred to something called artesian bread. I've looked everywhere and only found artesian water. Did you mean 'artisan' bread?" And here it came—the universal escape vessel for all "knowers," as Brené Brown calls them.[25] Without hesitation, he replied, "You can say it either way."

Well, no—you can't. They're spelled differently, have different meanings, and only one word and one pronunciation are appropriate for bread. *Artisan* is a craftsperson or describes handmade goods; *artesian* is water from a natural well. But she wisely decided not to attend the argument she'd just been invited to. It is unwinnable, and even if you could win, at what cost? He also tried to educate me on drilling in the Arctic and to educate Reneé on the medical field, claiming that he knew about drilling engineering and that he had read several medical journals. Later, I discovered you *can* say artesian for water and pronounce it like artisan—but you can't say artisan as artesian when you mean baked goods. At some point, you realize maturity isn't just knowing what you can change and what you can't; it's knowing what's not worth changing, even if you could. It's knowing that some people will never be self-aware enough to recognize that mistreating others creates distance. "Knowers" often label that distance as the other person's problem or loss.

Not every worthless argument involves knowers. Sometimes you're tempted into debates where you don't actually know enough to add value. The most powerful, classy, and disarming thing you can say is, "You know what? I don't really know enough about that to offer anything of substance, and I'd like to hear your thoughts."

It's hard to admit something like this. But authenticity is magnetic. People respect when you know what you don't know and you admit it. And for the record, politics and religion are still the fastest way to derail any conversation. They're polarizing, and most of the time, other people's opinions have zero impact on your life. Don't attend every argument you are invited to attend. And for goodness' sake, don't take a plus one.

Week 30

Be sensitive to the load everyone carries.

"He Ain't Heavy, He's My Brother"
—*The Hollies*

Life Lesson

Zig Ziglar nailed it decades ago in *See You at the Top*, and I'm paraphrasing here: "When you're at work, you want to be at home. When you're at home, you want to be at work, and you ain't never nowhere!"[26] Sound familiar? Most of us walk around with this vague sense of guilt that we're not giving 100 percent to anyone or anything. We feel like we should be doing *more*, being *better*, showing up *stronger*. And that guilt? It's just one more heavy item to carry.

Now imagine if everyone *could* see our burdens. Bob from accounting? He has an alarm bell going off and a baby monitor tucked in his pocket. Sheila from sales? She's hauling around student loan debt, an injured cat, and her ex's Netflix password. The guy in front of you in traffic, losing his mind over a blinker? He might just be carrying a load of grief and a broken AC. If we saw all that, *really* saw it, we'd probably be a lot slower to judge and a whole lot quicker to listen.

But here's the kicker: We don't. We often can't. So we assume. And when someone "goes off," we blame them, because we only see the behavior, not the baggage. As Stephen M. R. Covey said in *The Speed of Trust*, we judge others by their *actions*, and we judge *ourselves* by our *intent*.[27] That's why a quick text can land like a grenade. That snippy email? Maybe it wasn't snippy at all. Maybe it just *sounded* that way because of what's in your head at the moment. We read things through the lens of our own stress. And sometimes we create drama that doesn't even exist.

Everyone is carrying something: financial strain, aging parents, or just a nagging sense they're not enough. It's exhausting. And since we all have a load, we need to be careful with other people's hearts. Mel Robbins says in *The Let Them Theory* that people will do what they feel like doing.[28] And you know what controls what people feel like doing? You guessed it: that load we are carrying. Now what do we do?

Well, I start with real empathy, the kind that says, "Hey, are you okay?" and *means* it. You watch for clues, tone, posture, a sudden shift in someone's eyes. If someone pulls away mid-conversation, maybe it's not about *you*. Maybe the weightiness in their heart just got heavier. And when you mess up—and you will—*own it*. Say, "I totally forgot your dad just passed. I'm sorry I was being insensitive." That kind of humility? It's rare. And it matters. We all have blind spots. I'm a hardcore learner. I nerd out on leadership books and want everyone to be just as excited about a sixty-slide PowerPoint on emotional intelligence as I am (spoiler: they're not). So, when I'm teaching and someone pulls out their phone or looks at their watch, I have to fight the urge to take it personally. Maybe they're bored. Or maybe *I'm* off my game. Bottom line: Look for what is in their heart. And try not to add anything heavy to anyone else's pack.

The invisible backpack of life's stuff is a very anchoring concept to grasp, whether you are a parent, a sibling, a leader, a pastor, a business owner, or a bus passenger. We are all carrying something. I'm even good at imagining how things that are going well can get screwed up in case my backpack is feeling light.

I am wearing mine right now. And when I can see others wearing theirs, and sometimes I can, instead of the daily unfeeling question, "How're ya doing?" I ask, "Hey, you don't look like yourself today; is everything okay? Do you need a friendly ear?" It's strapped to your shoulders whether you are aware of it in the moment or not. And buddy, it's *full*. Cranky toddlers, guilt over not going to the gym (or going and immediately rewarding yourself with a dozen wings), or maybe a job you just can't get to because your mom is sick and your dad is losing his mind ... it's all in there. A little love can go a long way for all of us.

Week 31

Surround yourself with people who make you better.

"Better Together"
—Jack Johnson

Life Lesson

As you read through these stories, you're probably noticing I mention my mom and dad a lot. That's not by accident. For most of us, our parents, or some versions of them, are our original mentors. They're the first ones to teach us how to ride a bike, say please and thank you, and (if we're lucky) how to act when life knocks the wind out of us. But then comes the teenage phase. You know the one. It's the season of eye rolls and unsolicited wisdom that goes in one ear and out the other. Around fourteen, you're quite sure you've outgrown your parents intellectually. And fourteen-year-old daughters? Well, just order an exorcist for the spare bedroom. By the time you are eighteen, you're wondering how your parents ever figured out how to open a bank account or operate a microwave. Funny how that changes, isn't it? Somewhere along the way, maybe around age thirty, definitely by forty, we start to realize our parents weren't quite the idiots we thought they were. We were busy thinking we *invented* adulthood.

Still, I've always had people outside my family whose praise or advice seemed to hit a little differently. A teacher. A coach. A boss. A neighbor. It was someone who told me the truth when I needed it most. Their feedback felt more meaningful, not because it was better but because they *didn't have to say it*. They weren't obligated by blood. There's value in having a trusted third party who doesn't owe you a thing and chooses to invest in you anyway. Someone who listens without interrupting, challenges you without cutting you down, and speaks from experience rather than ego.

Social science agrees with this. Stephen Covey, in *The 7 Habits of Highly Effective People*, talks about the highest form of human relationship: interdependence.[29] That's when two people, both strong, both capable, choose to lean on each other, learn from one another, and grow together. We need those people. Trust isn't built by being perfect; Brené Brown says it's built by being real and by showing up with courage, vulnerability, and a willingness to care.[30] Simon Sinek, in *Leaders Eat Last*, says leaders create environments where people feel safe.[31] It's about putting people first, not just goals. The lesson is clear: Effective leadership, at work and at home, is built on real relationships, and real relationships are built on caring, respect, trust, and deep listening.

My dad always had a problem with the length of my high school hair. When I'd get home from the barber, he'd always say, "Looks to me like you left some change up there." Implying it was still too long. And that was in my "I hate my life" stage, moving so often that I had no friends. From fourteen to sixteen years old, I felt disenfranchised. Dad's disapproval didn't help. It was tough love, I guess. He didn't know how to help. I was too depressed for meaningful, honest conversations.

There is a hopelessness driven by raging hormones of the midteens when you lack Maslow's belonging. You are trapped in this short, gangly, pale, bad-haircut, disenfranchised, bone-aching pain. These were supposed to be the glory years. There was nothing glorifying about it.

Great relationships are built on trust, mutual respect, and a willingness to say the hard things the right way. I hadn't had that at home for a long time. My best mentors, the ones who made me better, didn't judge or tell me what to think. There were many. I had ministers and family friends who added perspective. They helped me learn *how* to think. They were empathetic and vulnerable, willing to listen. They asked questions like, "Interesting thought. How'd you get there?" "Have you considered another angle that might help you see it more clearly?" That's wisdom. That's mentorship. That's love without fluff. I've had those people in my life. And I'm grateful that, over time, my mom and dad became two of them. I lost them both in 2022, and their advice, once ignored, is now cherished. That's the thing about wisdom: It has a way of catching up to you. Hang on to those who challenge you *and* cheer for you.

The ones who make you feel safe enough to be vulnerable and strong enough to grow—they are gold. If the relationship is real, they'll learn from you too.

Week 32

Love people and use things, not the other way around.

"All You Need Is Love"
—*The Beatles*

Life Lesson

Years ago, I found myself at the intersection of two seemingly opposite goals: caring for people or producing business results. I had already seen firsthand that transactional leadership didn't inspire teams to go the extra mile. But I also knew that empathy alone wouldn't satisfy investors or clients. Something was missing. Coincident with attending graduate school and suffering from the linear way many HR leaders operate, I figured I could use my thesis project to fully understand the challenges and what the rest of the world thought of this dilemma. I decided to prove something radical: that caring and productivity are not in conflict; they are causal.

Over time, I developed a five-step leadership model with thirty-one elements of deep-dive social science behind the five. It began with something simple and often missing in leadership: caring. Not performative or policy-driven caring, but real, demonstrated concern for people's lives and futures. When I completed the literature search, which is part of discovering everything that has been written on the subject, I was convinced I was on to something. The greater discovery was not so much the necessity of caring; it was that all those brilliant leadership minds were holding themselves out as experts as if they had the magic bullet. They operated and studied in silos. Not only was their work interdependent, in their related thoughts, but it was also sequential. Until you understand the necessity of love in the workplace, you can't tackle the concept of respect, trust, self-awareness, relationships, and psychological safety. Until you master psychological safety, you will not be as successful introducing teamwork, determining the greater purpose of the work, goal setting, coaching for performance management, mastering check-ins, and focusing on the company productivity. The arrangement of these leadership elements in a logical flow from caring to business results forms a leadership framework, a model.

When this leadership model was applied across teams, something incredible happened: Business results improved across the board. In one case, employee turnover dropped by 50 percent over four years. In another, workers' compensation claims fell 85 percent, and recordable incidents were cut in half in a single year. We hadn't led with metrics. We had led with meaning. And the metrics followed.

Leadership isn't about choosing between people and performance. It's about understanding that one leads to the other. Too many executives treat caring as "nice to have," a luxury in hard times or a branding tool for good press clippings. But caring is the catalyst for clarity, commitment, and culture. It's the heartbeat of sustainable success.

Do your team members feel seen and known, not just managed?

Can people trust your consistency, even with discipline?

Do your leadership systems honor people or control them?

Encourage your staff and your heads of households to use things and love people, because loving things and using people is not the winning way.

Week 33

Be the person your dog thinks you are!

"Stand By Me"
—Ben. E. King

Life Lesson

I think my dogs are moderate Republicans. They don't share food. What they earn, they defend as theirs. They love everybody. They have luxurious spa days with blueberry facials included as a perk from their work. They are fully employed as canine doorbells and unarmed guards. They show signs of affluence as they love to announce the Amazon delivery. They are particular about where they do their business, and they make mistakes—and are unapologetic unless they get discovered. They earn their treats, and they do not share those either.

They move to the left at times. They have a bit of ACLU in them as they are good "people," believing in civil rights. Rylee, the Labrador, barks and jumps wildly to let us know when Bella, the Yorkie, gets accidentally locked in the pantry *unjustly*. They don't want to see other dogs detained or euthanized—they prefer adoption and birth control. They don't care what happens in other countries and don't watch the news.

There are more glimmers of being a "moderate." They do not call other dogs names or belittle their behavior record or make fun of their ethnicity. They are not jealous of other animal owners such as "childless cat ladies." But they are curious about them, smelling and examining them when they come around. They *do* sleep a bit when taking their meal breaks and rest breaks. They don't care about crowd sizes like presidential candidates do. They love every visitor, no matter how many or what ethnicity, gender, or sexual orientation. They do love Miss Adela who comes to clean twice each month. They know she is paid twenty dollars per hour—a fair wage—and do not ask if she is documented. She works harder than any American-born citizen. They donate their clothes and hand-me-downs to her. They have fictitious Petacare (fully paid medical) through their owner.

Here are some valuable lessons humans can learn from dogs.

Unconditional Love: Dogs show unwavering affection and loyalty to their owners, teaching us the importance of loving regardless of human affinities or opinions.

Living in the Moment: Dogs enjoy the present and simple things, reminding us to appreciate the "now." That fundamental of love shows up here. Short memories mean more joy.

Forgiveness: Dogs quickly forgive and forget, encouraging us to let go of grudges.

Resilience: Dogs often bounce back from adversity with a positive attitude, inspiring us to be resilient in the face of challenges.

Companionship: Dogs thrive on companionship and social interaction, highlighting the significance of building strong relationships.

Loyalty: Dogs are incredibly loyal to their families, reminding us of the importance of loyalty and trust in our relationships.

Empathy: Dogs are sensitive to human emotions and provide comfort, showing us the power of empathy and understanding.

A few years ago, our little Coco passed over the rainbow bridge. She had a tiny stuffed lamb that she cuddled. When she was gone, Bella, the Yorkie, who had barely acknowledged Coco, almost dismissing her at times, began acting strangely. She never cared for stuffed toys, or played fetch, or anything of the sort. One night, my wife called me into the bedroom. Bella was asleep, curled up on the bed with Coco's little lamb tucked underneath her paw. Sometimes we need to have remembrance and appreciate what we no longer have.

Be the person your dog thinks you are.

Week 34

Your children learn to love
from how you love.

"Forever and Ever Amen"
—*Randy Travis*

Life Lesson

Today is Father's Day. It's my third without either of my parents. I became an orphan in 2022, a grown man in my sixties, still feeling the sting of loss. We were close, even when separated by a continent at times. My dad was demanding and loving, a stern hand guided by a loyal heart. My mom was loving and instructional, full of wisdom and encouragement. I watched my father care for *his* father. I saw what love looked like, not the kind you say out loud. The kind you prove every day. I saw what being a *dad* really means. Because becoming a father is easy. Becoming a *dad*—that's something else entirely.

The bond with my boys changed over time. We've weathered challenges, and through it all, I loved them as my God-given legacy. Then, life surprised me again. When I married Reneé thirty years ago, I got two bonus children, daughters, under the age of nine who were missing an active dad. Loving them was instinct. Being their dad became one of the most rewarding privileges of my life. If you don't have stepchildren who need you, it is harder to relate.

It's a different kind of bond with the ones you choose, and it's no less powerful, and only subtly different. Either way, love doesn't come with conditions. Not in my house. When your kids are struggling—whether it's anxiety, depression, heartbreak, or divorce—you love them the same. I've become known for saying, "We're going to love you through this—and out the other side." That's what dads do.

This year, Father's Day feels extra special. First, my son Keaton, my Microsoft son, welcomed his first child with Dr. Kate—a beautiful miracle named Ashton Thomas Branch. It is Keaton's first Father's Day. Watching Keaton become a dad has been one of the great joys of my life. In him, I saw my father. I saw myself as a father, though I think he is better, deeply caring and even more available. I saw him rise to the role of servant leader in his home, not just in title but in action.

Later this year, my son Josh, who has long yearned to be a father, is marrying an incredible woman named Kristin. Kristin has two children, and Josh is already stepping in with tenderness, purpose, and strength.

He's doing what I did thirty years ago, loving children he is choosing. I could not be prouder.

On Father's Day Eve, Josh and I went to see James Taylor at Red Rocks Park and Amphitheatre in Colorado. It was a Father's Day gift for the ages. The crowd at Red Rocks was older, like me. Some attendees, gray and slow stepping, tackled the steep half-mile uphill walk with grit and grace. Josh stayed close, watched over me, and reminded me to take my time. It was subtle and caring. That circle of love—that's the legacy.

An aside of sorts ...

James Taylor's music has been a bond between my sons and me for decades. Keaton Taylor Branch is no coincidence. I told James Taylor that once. He smiled and humbly said, "You need to get a life!" It was perfect. This Father's Day weekend at Red Rocks Amphitheatre, James closed with my favorite song, "You Can Close Your Eyes," with his son, Henry, singing backup. I lifted my phone to record the moment. Josh gently reached over and said, "Dad, let me video. You just enjoy the song." He knew it was my favorite. The weight of the moment was of the unspoken.

We teach our children how to love, *not* with our lectures but with our lives. In the way we show up. In the way we listen. When they feel seen and heard, it is a safer place to be wrong and to ask the tough questions. I have been a dad for forty-seven years. I think I became the complete dad when I added stepchildren and especially because they are girls. No one warned me about the awkward teenage years of women. And we "loved them through it!"

At this moment, I am flying to my grandson's first birthday party tomorrow. I can't wait. When the times can be numbered that I will see him in my waning days, each one is precious. He will learn to love others in how we show up for him.

Week 35

Friendships are measured by tough times.

"You've Got a Friend in Me"
—*Randy Newman*

Life Lesson

It was somewhere around 1963. A group of our neighbors who became close friends over time would do what any middle-class family in Shreveport, Louisiana, would do in the summer: trek to Arkansas's Albert Pike Campground to the spring-fed clear rivers and the best camping cabins around. The kids would swim in the ice-cold water, walk across the river on the "rock bridges" made from piling a long line of rocks in the shallow water so you could walk from rock to rock and not get your tennis shoes wet. The older kids would go to the low-water bridge at night where some cigarette lighter powered a primitive boom box or a battery-powered "transistor radio" played loud enough that the music distorted. They would dance and make new friends with other teenagers.

One night a hysterical girl in the group came running up screaming, "Larry's dancing on the bridge!" What we had here was a situation! See, in my early childhood, as hard-core Southern Baptists, on paper we were against dancing, drinking, and smoking—and Larry was dancing! I found out later in life that aligning yourself with the most conservative end of the Christian spectrum only leads to deceit and other sleight-of-hand moves to hide the sinning. When the sun went down or they were off on vacation, particularly out of the country, the chains that bind fell off in a heap. Alcohol was kept in the farthest reaches of the home closet (which is the origin of being a "closet drinker"). We would see only the men smoking around the church and only outside the building in the breezeways. I don't remember seeing women smoking at church. Later in life, I joined the Church of Christ to align with my first wife's even more fundamental Christian beliefs. While there, one of the elders said in a Wednesday night classroom that dancing led directly to pregnancy, so dancing out of wedlock must be a sin. I am not anti-morals, but if you are going to cheat the system, at least don't pretend and don't thump your Bible while you are doing it. We weathered the "scandal" of Larry dancing on the bridge, and cooler heads prevailed.

Every night we camped, we built a fire and roasted marshmallows. On July 20, 1969, I watched the moon landing on a black-and-white

TV that sat on the hood of a car at that campsite. Days were filled with hikes to the spring where water would magically pour from the side of the mountain as if Jesus had commanded it. The friendships built in those days were and are lifelong. It was as if we had three or four sets of parents. Those memories of friends are indelible.

In a world that constantly measures success in dollars and possessions, we lose sight of the truth: The richest people aren't always the ones with the most money, but the ones with the deepest connections to others and the most meaningful memories. Think of the moments that fill your heart: the sound of your child laughing, a shared sunset with someone you love, an old friend showing up just when you need them. None of those can be bought or sold. They are earned, through time, with trust, love, and presence.

A lesson I've learned and seen lived by some of the wisest people I know is this: Money can buy things, but memories and relationships are what give life its meaning. When you measure your wealth by these, you'll never feel poor. You'll be surrounded by joy that doesn't depreciate, by friendships that weather time, and by stories that outlive you. Three of the "kids" from those days have passed away from various illnesses and accidents, and all except one of the parents are gone. Caroline, who goes by Carrie, my lifelong friend, is still in contact and came to my parents' funerals. What a gift. Ironically, after both of us living all over the continent and even, in her case, all over the world, now we live only two hours apart in Texas.

A friend said he was no longer giving gifts for birthdays. He is giving experiences to friends and family. He is demonstrating the "Albert Pike effect" by combining lifelong friends with experiences and emphasizing the true value of this life. He wants to be remembered for the life events and experiences he has created with others.

Those friendships are the kind you can depend on when things are not rosy. They are the ones who show up without being asked. About a year ago, my niece was struggling with a common wedding dilemma: whom to invite. The guest list felt overwhelming. She worried about offending someone, leaving someone out, or including people who didn't really matter. I gave her a piece of advice that's since resonated with others facing the same question: "When I think about the kinds of people I'd want at my wedding, I think about who I'd want there and, more importantly, who would show up at my funeral."

At first glance, that might sound morbid. But when you think deeply, it makes perfect sense. Many people happily attend a wedding. It's a celebration party, often a free-drink party for the guests. Some come out of joy and love; others come for the open bar. It's easy to show up when everything's going well. But funerals? People don't attend funerals for fun. They come out of love, loyalty, and deep respect. They come to mourn, to support, to honor a life that mattered. They come when it's hard. Those are the people I'd want to attend my wedding.

Most of us have been a plus-one at a wedding. But a funeral? That's different. If you've done that—stood beside someone simply so they wouldn't stand alone—then you are extra special. You are kind. You are loyal. You are a true friend. Life has a funny way of revealing our true circle, not in the good times but in the hard ones.

When you're unemployed and desperate for work, people don't always know what to say, so they avoid saying anything at all. When you're going through a divorce, your phone goes silent. The invitations stop. The awkward silences grow. When you lose someone close, people vanish, not out of cruelty but because they're unsure how to help. And then something magical happens: Someone unexpectedly shows up. Maybe they will send a card. Maybe they will bring flowers or a meal. Maybe they simply sit next to you and say, "You're not alone." They may not know the perfect words, but they're present. They show up. And when they do, you realize they weren't just acquaintances after all. They were friends. Real ones. You don't find your real friends in comfort. You find them in crisis. Real friends are the ones who step in when the world steps back. They see behind the mask, notice when you're not okay, and act, not with grand gestures but with calculating, unwavering presence.

Friendship isn't measured in how often you talk or how long you've known someone. It's measured in presence. In loyalty. In showing up when life is anything but easy. So, if you're wondering who to invite to your wedding—or who to call your friend—ask yourself this: *Who would come to my funeral?*

Want to build real wealth? Be there. Listen longer. Laugh more. Create moments that will echo in someone else's heart long after you're gone. I am the richest person I know, not because of material wealth but because of the abundance of love and support from longtime friends and colleagues. My life is filled with exceptionally talented people who are caring, driven, and meticulous leaders. My professional network is chock-full of resourceful, deep-thinking mentors and advisors. My wife and children are highly evolved humans who respect my life experience and enlighten me with their latest thinking. They help me grow through their own life navigation of the road less traveled.

Mitch Albom, in his timeless book *Tuesdays with Morrie*, says, "The way you get meaning into your life is to devote yourself to creating something that gives you purpose and meaning."[41] There is such peace and satisfaction where I am, even as I drive one of the world's smallest cars and eat dinner nightly with my wife on a TV tray. I am rich.

Week 36

Let people live in your heart.

"Heart of Gold"

—Neil Young

Life Lesson

Dick Lynn and I connected while I was at the Minute Maid Company, which at the time was a division of The Coca-Cola Company, headquartered in Houston, Texas. Dick was hired as a contractor to help with labor relations, and particularly for a sticky situation where employees were trying to decertify a union in a large plant. His home was Oklahoma City, which was my hometown for my high school years. Dick and I bonded over Oklahoma and the Houston Astros.

Dick went to Northwestern University where Milo Hamilton, the Major League Baseball Hall of Fame radio announcer of the Houston Astros, at one time called basketball games. Dick was Milo's analyst at the Northwestern games. An analyst is a person who keeps the statistics on the game and supplies them to the announcer. Dick went on to get his law degree from Northwestern.

Since Dick was tight with Milo and Milo commanded the radio booth for the Astros, Dick and I would get Milo's regular stadium seats to the games from time to time just below the radio booth. More than once, Dick got us into the radio booth with Milo. I have some great pictures. At the end of the game, Milo would stay behind and voice record commercials that would be placed at intervals in the next broadcast. We waited patiently until he finished, and then hugs and backslapping ensued.

Dick and I traveled the country doing union avoidance training, and then we logged many days as part of an effort to decertify a union in the Northeast and later a unionizing attempt at another plant. We will leave the name of the union and all individuals' names out of this text. Now I will tell you why.

See, that year, during union negotiations, a big black car pulled up next to me in a parking lot. The window rolled down just enough that the cigar smoke billowed from the window crack. A voice I did not recognize and similar to Darth Vadar told me I'd better watch my back and that neither I nor my family were safe. Let me just say that was the first and last time I ever had my life threatened in the line of duty, and it came straight out of a *Sopranos* scene. Upon receiving word of this threat, the company offered to provide twenty-four-hour surveillance of our house in Houston. I figured my house was so far away from where this was taking place in the Northeast that there was no need, and I declined. I didn't tell Reneé about that little incident until a decade later. I don't think she appreciated my decision to wait to tell her or to decline the protection. We ended up winning the decertification of the union, and nothing came of the threat on my life.

Dick was traveling with me on that trip, though not with me in the moment of the threat, and he guided me through the terror over dinner. When you go through situations like that with people, I suppose it is as close to going through a wartime battle as anything else as a civilian. Dick and I played golf and told HR stories. He was a great golfer. We are both under five-nine, but we were both known for hitting the ball three hundred yards on occasion. We were scrappers. Between the beers on the "nineteenth hole" talking about old Oklahoma City, the war stories we could tell about labor relations, and the nights at the Astros games, we became like brothers. Dick was fifteen years older than I was and had had a quadruple bypass when he was in his thirties. The doctors told him he'd be lucky to make it to fifty years old. When we were running around, I was not quite fifty years old, but Dick was in his early sixties with coal-black hair. He was in good shape with few wrinkles and a smile that lit up the room. He looked like he would live forever.

Coca-Cola decided to move the division that Dick and I worked for from Houston to Atlanta and consolidate it with the rest of Coca-Cola. Neither Dick nor I made the move, and both of us left the company. Dick and I parted business ways but stayed in touch. I was several years into my new job back in the oil business, but we continued to see each other and go to Astros games when he happened through town.

Dick was fascinated that I had begun playing music and singing in wine bars around town at that time. He pledged to come to one of my one-man shows. One particular night, I had a show and Dick was in town. He planned to go. At the last minute, he sent me an email saying that he was going to have to cancel on me and that he was so sorry to miss it. Then he said, "Play 'Walking Man' for me!" "Walking Man" is one of my favorite James Taylor songs. Dick knew I played a lot of James Taylor covers and assumed I played that song. It was the early days of me playing professionally, and that song was difficult for me then. I had not learned it, and I did not play it that night. It would be a few months before I realized how significant playing that song would become for the two of us.

A few months later, I got a call from Celine, a friend who had worked with Dick and me on some labor issues in the Northeast. I can still hear it, and it brings chills when I relive it. "Rod, I'm sorry, I wanted to make sure you knew that Dick died last night at his home in his sleep." He died on December 5, 2009, at the age of sixty-six. That is sixteen years longer than he was told he would live after the bypass. It was a devastating blow. And until my parents died, I hadn't had another person's death leave me so bone-crushing emotional. I'm not even sure I believe in this, but I feel his presence once in a while. I actually talk to him—out loud. It's eerie. But it feels real. This is another one of those situations that I am sure has a logical explanation, and we just don't know enough to explain it. I seem to get messages from him. I'm going to stop talking about that because I'm sure people will think I am crazy.

After hearing that news, I set about learning the song "Walking Man." It was partially a tribute to Dick and partially for me to work through the grieving process. I would sit down with the music, and I couldn't finish playing it. I could not get through the song in its entirety. I would get to the last few lines, and it just hit me in the center of my chest. You will see how the song ends. To this day, when I hear that song, I think of Dick. It would be several years before I could play it and sing it without falling apart. One line that always got me was, "Well now, would he have wings to fly? Oh, would he be free? Golden wings against the sky."[32]

Now, sixteen years later, I can play it and sing it. And I do it proudly for Dick. "Golden wings against the sky," my friend. Milo joined him in the heavenly broadcast booth six years later in 2015 at the age of eighty-eight.

I let Dick live in my heart, and I aways will. Sometimes we need those memories to comfort us. "So long, walking man, so long"!

Week 37

Invest in what you care about.

"If You Love Somebody Set Them Free"
—*Sting*

Life Lesson

My wife buys expensive sunglasses and keeps them for ten years. I buy cheap ones by the box and lose a pair a week. One day, I asked her, "How in the world do you manage not to lose those sunglasses? At those prices, I'd be living in a constant state of paranoia. That's why I stick with the cheap ones." Now, I should know better than to try to match wits with that woman. She calmly turned to me and said, "The reason I don't lose them is because they're expensive. The reason you lose yours is because they're seven dollars a pair." Touché.

She doesn't often wax philosophical, and when she speaks about the things she truly values, I've learned to listen. And she was right (again) about the sunglasses. It hit me later that I've owned a pair of name-brand sunglasses for over ten years now. Great optics. Comfortable. I keep them in my car and treat them with care. But when I'm out and about, I use the cheap ones, the ones I lose on restaurant tables or on the roof of my car. Without a purse or a set of cargo pants with an endless supply of pockets, those cheap ones vanish like single socks in the laundry. But here's the thing. If I *valued* them like I do my wallet or credit cards, I wouldn't abandon them. That's the sunglasses principle: We take care of what we value. We track it. We protect it. We prioritize it.

Take a moment. Think about what's profoundly important to you. Write those things down. Then next to each one, write how much time or attention you *actually* give it. Now ask, *Does any of this make sense?*

I say I value my personal health. I say I value time with family. But then I look at how many hours I spend at work, writing this book, traveling, responding to email, and I realize the correlation is there. The *proportion* is off. No one will care if this book gets finished three months late. But my kids will care if I delay three months in visiting them or skip out on time when they're in town. Now, in fairness, this book feeds my love of learning, so in some ways I'm solving two equations at once. But if I'm being honest, I could still do more to align my *time* with my *values*. Instead of collapsing in front of a mindless show at the end of the day,

I could be walking, riding my bike, working in the garage, or just calling someone I love.

Stephen Covey, in *The 7 Habits of Highly Effective People*, wrote about "first things first," where he maps tasks by *urgency* and *importance*.[33] The challenge lies in what's "important but not urgent." That's the self-care, the planning, the relationships, the things that matter most in the long run, and rarely shout the loudest.

So now, when I face a decision, I ask these questions:

- *What's the worst thing that can happen if I don't do this?*
- *Who wins or loses?*
- *Will ignoring this now create a bigger problem later?*

If I treat something like cheap shades as a low priority, whether it's a task, a person, or even my health, it usually falls by the wayside. But if it matters to me, I will track it. I protect it. I show up for it. Just like those expensive sunglasses. Someone wise once said, "Use things and love people. Never get those backward." So maybe it's time we reassign value, away from convenience and toward connection. Away from urgency and toward intentionality. Value what matters. Invest where it counts.

Never lose sight of the things you can't replace.

Week 38

Trust but verify.

"Suspicious Minds"
—Elvis Presley

Life Lesson

In the fall of 2024, my adorable niece Maura asked me if I would officiate her wedding. I was honored. A few years earlier, I had gotten ordained, somewhat on a challenge, by my friend Cindy at an insurance carrier dinner. Right there, we went online, and I got ordained by answering a few questions and sending for the certification card and some blank ceremonial wedding certificates. It also came with a "Clergy" placard for the rearview mirror to allow you to park in clergy parking at the hospitals. I never used that privilege until my mom was in the hospital for so long and the disabled parking was always full. I had to get my dad closer to the building.

As I was included in some of the planning for the wedding, we began to focus on the lakeside venue near Orlando, Florida. First, the weather that time of year in Orlando would be about 95 degrees and about 70 percent humidity. We prayed it would not rain.

Secondly and more importantly, I discovered that this beautiful body of water, Lake Jessup, had more alligators per unit of water than any lake in Florida. In fact, alligators are rescued and relocated from other neighborhoods and lakes to Lake Jessup. It is a kind of purgatory for alligators, and they are cranky and are having none of it. The lake is in view of and behind the wedding venue and is separated from people by a poorly maintained wire fence. With the traditional wedding positioning and all the seating facing the lake, I was the only one at this wedding who could not see the lake during the entire service. I had to turn my back to the angry crowd at Gator Lake. I had to trust the audience to tell me if there was a future pair of boots coming up the walk from the crowded waters. Could I trust them to do that?

As I reflected on that wedding venue story, I began to put it in perspective. People are different at work than at home. That isn't always bad. But it is bad often enough that HR gets referred to as adult babysitting, a well-earned title. Human resources as a profession is much like working near an alligator-infested swamp. We have a sea of personalities, personal histories, and dispositions. Most people can behave in a normal range at the office, provided they are not overly stressed, inebriated, or have something in their backpack that is controlling their feelings. The career is designed to make you expect the worst in people, at least until you come to grips with the concept of situational leadership.

HR professionals can tell HR trust-related stories from our businesses only to other HR professionals at HR happy hours. We can't discuss the behaviors of our employees with employees at the office. Those are confidential. Happy hour is the only safe place to discuss some of the behaviors we encounter, and only if we leave the names of the people out. I've had employees take hamburgers that were left over from a company party. Someone took small single-package dessert cakes from a coworker's desk. Then, someone was "taking" packets of sugar from the coffee area by the fistfuls—really? A spoonful of sugar costs about two cents. We pay well enough so that people can buy sugar. If we can't trust them with the sugar, how do we trust them with company assets? This is about the surprising behavior of unsupervised workers. It's hard to know who you can trust.

So here is a practice that has merit and works much of the time. I teach relationship building constantly. It is hard to lie to or steal from someone with whom we have a good working relationship. Offsite events, lunches, and coffee talk—i.e., occasions where people can let their guard down and start building vulnerable relationships—will build trust. The cost of a poor working relationship is trust. We learn not to blindly trust people who have not earned our trust. Let people earn your trust.

Week 39

Recognition is something afforded those who already are known.

"Respect"
—*Aretha Franklin*

Life Lesson

About once a week in my role as chief human resources officer, I get a message from a magazine offering to feature me as "Most Dynamic CHRO" or as one of the "Top 100 HR Professionals." It usually promises a glowing feature story, an electronic badge for social media, a press kit to circulate across wire services, and, of course, print copies of the magazine with me on the cover. They make it sound like a real honor. Enticing, right? Who doesn't want to be seen and celebrated? Then I read further. The "recognition" comes at a price. They actually charge you a fee, usually between $1,500 and $3,500. Suddenly, it doesn't feel like an award. It feels like advertising and vanity, paid self-promotion disguised as merit. And the truth is, people can smell the difference. As my friend Janean says, "Who in the actual hell does that?" I would not even want that as a gift from my team. It is icky.

I once worked with a CIO who fell into that trap. She paid for one of these features and left a stack of magazines on her conference table, the cover boasting the CIO's name and the phrase "CIO of the Year." It became the talk of the office, but not in the way she had hoped. The whispers weren't admiration. There were eye rolls. Of course, the desire behind it is human. We all want attention. We want to be seen and heard. We want to matter—to be connected, appreciated, and valued. Maslow taught us that. And like many others, I've felt the ache of being unseen.

I knew early in my career that I wouldn't be the smartest engineer on the rig. But I could be the hardest-working one. I wasn't the slickest lobbyist either, but I was eager to learn. For the first fifteen years in HR, even up to enrolling in graduate school in my late fifties, I never thought recognition was something attainable. I wasn't chasing titles; I wasn't ready for them either. I doubted my confidence, my influence, and my ability to lead at the vice president level. I was, as I called it, "the best number two in the company." And I had resigned myself to that role. Until one day, my wife challenged that resignation.

She said, "You are smart enough and socially aware enough to handle that next level. You just haven't asked for the opportunity." She was right—again. I had never *asked* for a promotion. Every role I had ever taken was something someone offered. I had never initiated the ask. So I did. I asked the CEO for a shot. I even used another VP as a benchmark to make my case. There was another VP of HR in another division who was less qualified than I was and had a much smaller division than mine, yet he was already a VP. The CEO gave me the chance. And I was right about one thing: I wasn't ready. I was underconfident and underprepared, but I was no longer passive. What followed was not a crash. It was a climb.

Graduate school taught me how employees become business assets by feeling valued, liking their manager, and doing work that aligns with the company's purpose. I became obsessed with helping others become great leaders who in turn build strong teams and grow future leaders of their own. In *Ego Is the Enemy*, Ryan Holiday says, "Ego blocks us from improving by telling us we don't need to improve. What is rare is not raw talent, skill or even confidence; it is humility, diligence, and self-awareness."[34] Success isn't found in manufactured recognition. It's found in steady growth, fueled by gratitude, curiosity, and the relationships we invest in. If we pursue big goals through small actions, learning, and giving more than we take, recognition will simply confirm what others already know. Confidence isn't a title. It's a mindset. And as it turns out, confidence can't be purchased for $3,500 and a magazine cover.

Week 40

Things are never as good or as bad as they seem.

"Both Sides Now"
—Joni Mitchell

Life Lesson

Even a bad hair day can be fixed with a hat. Malcolm Gladwell's ideas in *Blink* contrast with other decision-making theories in several ways. He talks about thin slicing, where people make quick, intuitive judgments based on limited information.[35] This contrasts with rational decision-making models, like Daniel Kahneman's concept of *Thinking, Fast and Slow*, which distinguishes between fast, instinctive thinking and slow, deliberate reasoning.[36]

After thirty-five years working in government affairs and human resources and a few years studying people in a graduate program, I've learned that to resolve conflicts we need to ask, "What do we know for sure?" We must focus on clear facts and avoid emotional storytelling to understand what was said, meant, and understood.

Our first reaction is dictated by the call center in our brain, known as the amygdala. The amygdala takes the calls from the sensors and dispatches the reactions to other parts of the body. It happens so fast that the amygdala must operate on an immediate interpretation of facts, whether there is extensive information or a cursory set of data. It is instinctive and innate. Then we have the more rational sections of the brain where real data is processed and reactions are measured and assigned. Okay, that was way too much science for what we need here.

In the face of shocking news like Reneé's cancer diagnosis, many of us expect the worst. In the face of good news, many overexaggerate the good news, perhaps bragging, and falsely assign a more favorable impression than is warranted. As a consequence, we must moderate our emotions, take a breath, assess the situation, and form a constructive reaction. Things are rarely as good or as bad as they seem.

Gladwell's work is fascinating because it highlights the power of instinct while cautioning against its pitfalls. Books like *Think: Why Crucial Decisions Can't Be Made in the Blink of an Eye* by Michael R. LeGault challenge Gladwell, advocating for more deliberate, logical decision-making.[37] We need both, depending on whether or not we are in immediate danger.

When I didn't get the promotion to my first vice president role, I initially felt it was a significant setback. But over time, I realized that this experience pushed me to seek opportunities that I wouldn't have considered otherwise. I was missing some business context and a heap of balancing between what employees wanted and what the business needed—and the implied tightrope that lay between the two. Getting the promotion might have come with unanticipated challenges and stress.

When Reneé received her cancer diagnosis and a round-trip ticket to MD Anderson Cancer Center, we were resolved to change whatever part of our lives needed adjustment to give us both a better chance at a longer life. Healthier foods, exercise, and cutting back on recreational drinking were in plain view and doable. And while her clean bill of health—the great news that the cancer had not spread and they'd gotten it all—made lifestyle changes seem less dire or necessary, we doubled down and are now using it as a slingshot to better health.

The end of a relationship can likewise feel like the end of the world, yet it often leads to personal growth and the opportunity to find a more compatible partner. Conversely, starting a new relationship can be exciting, and it also requires effort and compromise to maintain. These examples show that our initial reactions to events can be extreme, and with time and perspective, we often find that the reality of eventual outcomes is more balanced—never as bad or as good as we first imagine. Start with, "What do we know for sure?" While the story we tell ourselves might be comforting, it may not be the facts we need in the moment. It's not just about avoiding Pollyanna, rose-tinted thinking; it's about mitigating doom-and-gloom overreactions too. In fact, the doom-and-gloom overreactions are far more dangerous than being too hopeful.

Part IV — Legacy and Transcendence

Becoming Someone to Someone

Every journey ends with new meaning. Legacy and transcendence are the season of reflection—the recognition that what matters most is rarely measured in numbers, titles, or trophies. It's measured in the lives we touch, the wisdom we share, and the love we leave behind.

This section invites you to slow down and take stock of the story you're writing with your life. It's about gratitude, generosity, and the velvet grace of letting go. Here, legacy is not a monument to yourself; it's a bridge to others.

In the end, leadership is about being *felt* in the hearts of those who carry your kindness forward. Legacy, after all, is about being someone to someone.

Week 41

Accept the love and generosity of friends and family.

"Bridge Over Troubled Water"
—*Simon and Garfunkel*

Life Lesson

I just got a message from a neighbor, a beautiful single young mom who was widowed after a tragic accident in our neighborhood. Three young, smart, talented fathers/husbands/sons, who were neighbors and friends, were killed on a golf cart, hit by an Escalade going seventy miles per hour in a forty miles-per-hour zone and blowing through a stop sign. The oldest victim was in his early forties, and the other two were in their thirties. The day was two years ago as I write this. Just devastating. Recently, our friend Somer, one of the widows, posted on Facebook that she was having a tough day, describing it as "juggling fire while riding a unicycle." No words can erase the harsh memory or the pain left in the heart. Nothing can be said to "fix" it. But the human spirit seems to respond well to empathy. We can define empathy as intellectually understanding how another person might feel, even if we can't truly feel what they feel.

To express empathy, we must start with genuine caring. Then from there we learn to show respect, mostly through generous listening. Then we build trust. Trust enables vulnerability and empathy. Our vulnerability and empathy enable others to feel safe sharing feelings without being judged and compels us and others to admit when we have wronged someone or we've made a mistake.

When I read Somer's post, having also just gotten the news about Reneé's uterine cancer diagnosis, I began to tear up. I felt something for her situation, struggling to regain her true self and navigating life without her "life mate." When we experience a loss, many will reach out with well wishes and offer to have you call them if you need anything. You never call. They are well-meaning. We must remember that their sentiment and commitment are real. They mean it. Often, they just don't know what good help looks like to you, so they are at a loss. Sometimes you don't know either.

People who are truly empathetic will have an idea what makes things better. It isn't that they know; it is that they "do." Unsolicited, they show up with a basket of flowers, cookies for the kids, or a hot pot of coffee and two mugs. They "do" without asking. And over coffee, they may say the wrong thing. They are not trained therapists or psychiatrists, and their hearts are in the right place. Tell yourself that they went out of their way, bought and brought gifts, and took time out of their busy life to attend to you! You have no obligation to share about your struggles. Just lean into the unsolicited love outpouring and accept it as a gift.

I try to tell myself that most people are well-intended. I don't think many people who behave badly wake up and say, "How can I jack up someone's life today?" It could be what is in their invisible backpack that is causing them to act out. We never know completely how someone else is struggling. Fortunately, or unfortunately, I have stood in six different living rooms of family members whose loved ones were killed at work—on my HR watch. Everyone "hates on" the HR guy until one of those situations comes along. Then *no one* wants that job. Everyone in those living rooms looks at you as the representative of the company that just took their loved one and torpedoed their lives. It is hard for them in the moment to understand that you really do care and that you want to help. These days, after being on the losing end in many of these situations, I feel more comfortable saying something or doing something unsolicited to help, even if it won't be appreciated. As I mentioned earlier in week 15, we must approach the awkward or misguided but well-intentioned goodwill gestures with understanding and a willingness to see their caring heart.

When I responded to Somer about her comment that life was like juggling fire while riding a unicycle, I was empathetic. I told her that no one can understand completely the devastation she has endured. I reminded her of the words from both Sheryl Crow and Coldplay.[39] They both have lyrics in hit songs that remind us we're never promised life would be easy or warned that it would be this hard.

Somer and I have a bond regarding my music. Her father-in-law, Stu, who lost his son, had heard me play on my dock from Somer's house, which is about forty yards from mine across the water. Stu hired me to play for an event he was sponsoring at his community center in his neighborhood. We became instant friends. It was only weeks before the accident. It was the music that connected Somer, Stu, and me. Since the accident, Somer asked me to play for a family gathering she was hosting. She wanted to pay me to play. I asked if this was to be at her house, and she said no, she wanted me to play from my own dock so the neighbors could hear. Of course, I agreed to play, but as long as I live, the least I can do is to play the music that binds our families—and for Somer and Stu, there will never be a fee.

Week 42

Limitations don't define you.

"Defying Gravity"
—*Wicked* cast

Life Lesson

This is a book containing many stories of overcoming adversity. You can tell by the long string of risen phoenixes in my lineage that I made a lot of mistakes but had some little victories too. Most of us have done something early in our lives that we regret. Then we spend the rest of our lives proving we've recovered or made amends. Let's reach back about a century and see one of the great survivors of missteps in my family.

My mother's dad, Elmer—again, a grandfather with no middle name—was short. At maybe five foot six, he earned the nickname "Shorty" somewhere along the way. Shorty's father and brother were both six feet or better, broad men with big frames, yet Elmer carried just as much presence, if not more. I never knew much about Elmer's father, other than he was known to bare-knuckle box on weekends in the streets of Lake Charles, Louisiana, to earn extra money. His name was John Foreman, and his work was to manage floating logs on the Calcasieu River to transport them to the sawmill. That image always stayed with me, a man gritty and fearless, fighting for a little more. Elmer had some grit of his own.

As a teenager, Elmer had a run-in with a blasting cap, those little detonators used to set off bigger explosives like dynamite. The accident cost him most of his index finger, about half his middle finger, and a good portion of his thumb. By the time I came along, that's just how I knew him. It never seemed strange. It was simply part of who he was. He, too, was a scrapper. Missing fingers never slowed him down. He operated heavy equipment, delivered telegrams, worked as a Ford mechanic, was a tankerman and tugboat pilot, and ran operations in a Lake Charles refinery. I once watched him twirl a screwdriver in his compromised hand like any other fully digited man. You'd never guess he was operating with net eight fingers because he lived life at "eleven." His self-inflicted setback in life was no deterrent; rather, it was likely more of a propellant.

Shorty was an avid reader. With a formal education of only seven grades, he felt obligated to make up the difference in self-study. He especially liked animals of all kinds. He knew all the different types of birds, spiders, and other critters, and kept books on them near his chair. He was also a bit of a tinkerer and an early MacGyver. When he needed a tool he didn't have, I saw him use a grinder or punch or sledgehammer, and a new tool would appear. With pure curiosity and some automotive education, he built a tow-behind trailer out of a truck bed to haul garbage to the city dump. Hanging on the garage wall was the largest magnet I'd ever seen, two feet across and heavy as a boat anchor. He stored his screwdrivers, punches, and drill bits on it, and screws clung to the tools, making projects easier. Elmer invented efficiency and was doing lean manufacturing long before it was a Six Sigma fad in America. He also might be one of the original recyclers. He never threw away a bread bag. In southwestern Louisiana, where the marsh kept everything damp and moldy, bread bags kept tools and supplies dry. He cut Clorox jugs into scoops for salt for softening the water from the well. He didn't waste. He repurposed.

Shorty has made one of life's long-used axioms indelible for me: Necessity is the mother of invention. I suspect his modest living and hard work at the plant often left him with a need that demanded fulfillment. He could imagine a solution in his head and then went to his workshop to make it come true. Once when I was little, I saw him cut the bottom off a plastic dish soap bottle, attach a copper tube to the plastic nozzle, turn it upside down, and pipe the condensation from our window unit air conditioner away from the driveway to prevent the slick concrete from getting wet. Genius! He once was helping me with a dangling tooth as a young boy. He tied a string to the tooth and then tied the other end to a doorknob in his house. As he was tying the string to the doorknob, he gave the string a quick jerk as I was waiting patiently for the string to be tied to the doorknob. The tooth popped right out. I learned that bar soap was a lubricant for a zipper that wasn't cooperating and that tapping a stuck jar lid all around the edges would loosen the lid.

Elmer lived a full, capable, city-boy life and retired with his house and land paid off. He did 100 percent of his life with 80 percent of his fingers. He never mentioned his missing fingers. Never complained. Never used it as an excuse. After a while, nobody else noticed either.

This is another story about perseverance. My grandfathers had no opportunity to get a formal education. Wallace, my paternal grandfather, had a setback with being locked down by the sharecropping imprisonment. Elmer had to overcome losing the use of a lot of his hand. Both were successful: Wallace as a small-business owner and Elmer as a long-term refinery worker with a good pension and some cash in the bank. While their body of knowledge was different, they both became well-educated in how to navigate this world. In many ways, way better than I did—Wallace with a hoe and Elmer with endless curiosity about everything. Both scrappers. Both resilient.

Week 43

Keep the music in you.

"Listen to Your Heart"

—Roxette

Life Lesson

It is fascinating how the short years and long days are spent raising kids, attending dance recitals and school plays, buying prom attire, moving them to college, and then continuing to support them for years after that. Where does the time go? I have been richly blessed; despite some mild hearing loss, slightly high cholesterol, and a life of serial migraines, I am otherwise reasonably healthy. I can still play gigs at bars and restaurants, weddings and funerals, and occasionally fireside crooning. However, with kids in Denver and Houston, and grandkids all the way to Seattle, I have slowed my music commitments to make room in my schedule for them.

Louis Armstrong once said, "Musicians don't retire; they stop when there is no more music in them." Back in 2006, I was playing for free in bars, off-key at times but always on purpose. A loyal circle of friends kept showing up, even when the music wasn't good. That encouragement kept me going. In later years, after forty-two gigs in a single year, my voice matured, and I could reach notes I once only admired. I never lost the desire to make music, though today it's more likely to echo in the solitude of my Bourbon Room than from a stage. My schedule may be lighter, but the music hasn't left me.

Returning to school in my late fifties felt like tuning a long-silent instrument. Overcommitted and overjoyed, I dove into leadership studies and wrote a thesis that transformed how I saw the world. My advisor once told me, "If you do this right, you'll know more about your thesis subject than anyone on the planet." I smiled politely, secretly skeptical. But soon I was holding my own in high-level conversations, growing into a voice in the field of leadership.

That experience unlocked something bigger than credentials. Over the next two years, I led HR for a company of six thousand people, read over a hundred books on leadership, and began speaking nationally at conferences. Leadership stopped being my job; it became my music. But more importantly, I learned the most powerful harmony comes when you lead with love. Caring is what turns a leader into someone others want to follow. Just like music, caring is an instrument, one that makes life richer, relationships deeper, and conflict more navigable.

We spend our lives searching for meaning, reading *The Alchemist*, chasing *The Secret*, praying the melody we're chasing is the right one. The leadership model I developed, a central theme of a future book, turned out to be more than a business tool. It applies to marriage, culture, safety, coaching, and even labor relations. It feels like the secret sauce of life. And it's still playing in me.

But here's the twist: I discovered my perfect career at fifty-nine. It's like being handed the keys to a brand-new 747, then realizing the runway ahead may not be long enough to get it off the ground. That's why I intend to keep flying and to extend the runway as long as I can. At sixty-seven, I see now that life's crescendo isn't found in titles, accolades, or even flawless performances. It's in grace. It's in letting people speak from their invisible backpack of burdens without judgment. It's in kindness for kindness' sake. It's in forgiving quickly and choosing peace. That's the music in me now. And maybe that's the music in you too. So I ask again, do you still have the music in you? And can your chosen music "save your mortal soul"?[40]

Week 44

Wisdom is earned, not gifted.

"The Long and Winding Road"
—The Beatles

Life Lesson

Lately, I've found myself in conversations with twenty- and thirty-somethings explaining the meaning of words like "doily." That somehow opened the floodgates. Next thing I knew, we were time-traveling through the gasoline lines of the '70s, Watergate, where I was when Kennedy was shot, and the fact that Martin Luther King Jr. was killed on my tenth birthday. They blinked like I'd just described a black-and-white movie. Which, ironically, led us to black-and-white television, what a smudge pot was, how clotheslines were a thing, and how hot plates were practically gourmet gadgets. That's when I realized: I've become the walking, talking throwback channel. And you know what? I kind of love it.

It hit me that this must be how my dad felt when explaining how his family preserved cooked sausage in a barrel of lard during the summer. No fridge, just fat and faith. "If air can't get to it, it won't spoil," he'd say with pride. He came from a time when hitchhiking was transportation, not a cautionary tale.

I still remember the day I helped my dad connect his stereo to wired speakers using RCA cables, feeling like a tech wizard. Fast-forward a few decades, and now I'm the one calling my son to figure out how to talk to the house just to turn the lights on. Somewhere between analog and Alexa, we all evolved.

Each generation gets its own set of gadgets, oddities, and stories. And each leaves something behind the next won't even know existed. It's not bad; it's just the rhythm of time.

When I was thirteen and my family moved to Oklahoma City, I was the new kid, completely out of sync. They put me in a class with the A/V nerds who ran the school's film projectors. Yes, film. The term *movie* was short for "moving pictures" literally. I became a pro at threading reels, splicing and gluing breaks, and fixing sound with a magical little thing called an exciter bulb. It was the light that read the portion of the film that carried the signals for synchronous sound. This whole A/V thing rang my reclusive bell. I didn't have to talk to anyone.

I didn't have to introduce myself to anyone. This was a skill, this A/V thing, but it would never come in handy later, I thought.

Years later, in college, I was in a physics class in a huge classroom—hundreds of students. This particular class period, they were trying to show a film about the moon. The team of people were gathered around the projector because the sound would not play. When I turned around to look at the commotion, I recognized the RCA-brand projector in the back of the class and knew immediately what was wrong. I yelled, "Flip the exciter switch!" The projection team looked lost and clearly didn't know what I was talking about. So I walked to the back, located and flipped the switch, and boom, we had sound. For one brief, shining moment, I was the hero nobody knew they needed. My inner Napoleon Dynamite nerd did a victory dance. In high school, I read survival books that taught ancient skills such as starting fires, purifying water, building shelters. It amazed me how brilliant past generations were. They didn't have less intelligence, just fewer and more primitive tools.

My childhood TV was a huge brown wooden box with steel legs and exactly zero remotes. I was the remote. Breaking news was about a week old, and somehow we still survived. Now I can watch live footage from across the globe on my phone before I finish my morning coffee.

What's the point of all this vintage rambling? Simple: If you want to stay relevant, keep learning new things. If you want to stay wise, don't forget the old things. Every generation has something to teach and something to learn. We're all just passing the torch, sometimes in the form of a cassette tape, sometimes a smart speaker. And here's the good news: The more you know about the past, the more you can laugh about the present, and the more ready you'll be for whatever the future throws your way.

Week 45

You don't know what you've got till it's gone.

"Big Yellow Taxi"
—Joni Mitchell

Life Lesson

Joni Mitchell's song "Big Yellow Taxi" has that famous line: "You don't know what you've got till it's gone."[41] If you're talking about dating in high school, it feels like the end of the world at the time. Breaking up is devastating with young love. But the wounds heal eventually; you move on, and life teaches you that these emotional setbacks are survivable.

As you get older, the stakes rise. Long-term relationships aren't just about romance; they're woven into your soul like a quilt, with children, shared memories, and a lifetime of experiences. The investment is deep emotionally, and there is a gravitational pull with the relationship that causes you to consider the memories, the children, even those step-children who have become like biological children, and all the financial implications. There is more motivation to stay together.

For Reneé and me, it is the second time around for both of us. With her two girls and my two boys, we found each other quickly after our first marriages. The boys were sixteen and nine years old and the girls were eight and barely four. The boys' mom had some difficulty with depression for most of the last nine years of our seventeen-year marriage. She needed to take care of herself and moved back to Oklahoma. I took care of the boys in Texas. The girls had some relationship with their dad, most of it spotty and seemingly not very close. As a result, we inherited a project of raising this clan of now four children ranging from four to sixteen years old full-time together, and I traveled to Capitol Hill or state capitols several times each month. I ended up switching to human resources from government affairs for more time at home, and we set about surviving this new family arrangement. There were stressful times, and our May-to-December romance from an arranged meeting to sliding rings on was quick. No one thought it would last. We wondered at times.

Reneé worked from home running a medical transcription business for a prominent breast oncologist so she could flex her schedule to do the kid care. Reneé and I traveled to Europe for my work a couple of times. The girls had never been out of Texas or taken a real vacation, so we took the younger three kids to Rodeo Drive in Los Angeles for a week, and once, we were fortunate enough to go to Hawaii and take all the kids with us.

On our journey, we supported each other going back to college, Reneé becoming a nurse and me legitimizing my VP of HR title with a master's in global HR. Reneé had a couple of major surgeries, neither particularly life threatening but both with long recoveries. I started playing music, gigging for parties and a few wine bars and breweries. She came to every show and has heard me play "Fire and Rain" a thousand times between my rehearsals and performances. She is a saint. At the shows she would work the room, greeting everyone and knowing that it was the draw of the crowd that got me invited back for the next show. We have had a full life. She lost her parents young, being the caboose of her family of origin, and we cared for my parents who retired about the time we got married. We traveled with them to Ireland and Scotland. My dad was particularly fun in Europe, and my mom liked to drink whiskey—which made her extra fun. They became her parents too. Reneé and I do everything together, so much so that when I travel to places she has not been, I feel strange experiencing those places alone. *Where is my traveling buddy?* There is always an emptiness.

We were also resilient. We rode the eight-second ride of the oil and gas business, going through layoffs seemingly annually. We sought the stability of the non-oil-and-gas Coca-Cola Company, only to weather the largest class action race-based lawsuit in history to that point. We then survived a thousand-employee "reduction in force" and declined to move with the rest of the business from Houston to the Coke mothership in Atlanta. We leaned heavily on each other. We were one.

After thirty years, we didn't know how to do "life" without each other.

It was June 2, 2025, at 1:58 p.m. I was at work in northwest Houston when I got the text from Reneé: "Looks like my good luck just ran out. Just got the call about my biopsy. I'm being referred to MD Anderson." MD Anderson is a world-renowned cancer center here in Houston. In all my years, I'd never received a text message like that. Neither of us nor any of our kids had suffered serious accidents, illnesses, or afflictions. And now—cancer?

She's had some scares before, and each time the results came back negative. I had assured her that luck was always on our side. What did I know? But in this situation, I needed to be the "chief hope officer" of the family. She had lost all her older siblings, and there was no one except our family to support her.

It felt almost ironic. Just this past winter, I'd learned to play and sing Elton John's deep track "Believe." One of its best lines is "War makes money, cancer sleeps."[42] Well, we'd just poked the hibernating bear. In an instant, your mind resets. You start imagining the empty chair. You think about future vacations, dinner parties, weddings, and birthdays—and where you might find yourself alone. And the kids without their mom—wow!

As a DiSC "i," an influencer, I live for relationships, optimism, and enthusiasm. When Reneé works late at the hospital, in those couple of hours alone I feel incomplete. So imagining life without her is impossible.

We decided with the surgeon's permission to go on a trip to Lake Placid, Montreal, and Vermont. We had a wonderful time, but always in the fog of this heavy cloud. On July 14, 2025, Reneé had a hysterectomy by a robot named DaVinci. A name that seems pompous. To remove all the no-longer-functioning parts that might contain cancer she had to have the anatomical equivalent of five bullet holes in her abs. Ouch!

We were promised a pathology report within fourteen days. At her post-op appointment ten days in, the surgeon said they were having to do some additional stains on the tissue samples and that it was delaying the results of the pathology report. Reneé, being a nurse and having worked twenty years for an oncologist, knew that more stains was not good news. We were promised results on the 23rd—but no call. I stayed home from work the next day and then the next, just in case, so she wouldn't be alone for the call. And no call. No call over the weekend. We were a mess. Worry is too small a word.

Then, on July 28, 2025, at 11:27 a.m., she got the call at work: "All clear." No cancer. We caught it early, it didn't spread. Nothing in the lymph system.

That was a reason to celebrate!

After thirty exciting and sometimes crazy years together, our love looks different than it did in our thirties. These days, it's lived out as traveling companions, TV-tray dinner partners, and fellow Netflix binge-watchers. We like the same kinds of people, we're reasonably healthy other than the cancer scares, and we are, as Paul McCartney sang, "things that go together well."[43]

But here's the question: Why does it take the threat of losing something or someone we love to make us act the way we should every single day? Well, because loss hits harder than gain. We live life looking forward and only fully understand it looking backward. In hindsight, memories gloss over the difficulties and highlight the good. They carry more meaning than our forward-looking daydreams. When a doctor tells a lifelong runner, "I think you should give up running," it's devastating—believe me, I know. It feels final. In our teens and twenties, we think we're going to live forever. But somewhere along the way, we learn better.

Look at what you have.

Thank the heavens.

I appreciate the color in flowers, the flavor of a great steak, and the magic of tight harmony in songs and in life.

Be present.

Live fully.

And don't wait until it's almost gone to see and say how much people and life mean to you.

Week 46

Don't wait for the perfect time to pursue your dreams and desires.

"Don't Stop Believin'"
—*Journey*

Life Lesson

It was June 12, 2024. My friend Kyla, an HR professional in the oil and gas business, passed away suddenly of natural causes at fifty-two years old. As I sat with friends at the funeral, hearing her high school children talk of the exciting things planned that their mom would not get to experience, I thought to myself, *What if this were me instead of her?*

There is so much I have not done. There are so many apologies—so many amends to make. There are experiences that Reneé I have in the planning books and are waiting for the right bank deposit or time in our worldly busy schedules to squeeze it in. I'm sure Kyla would have spent her last days much differently had she known. I'm sure she is looking down on all of us now and saying, "Get 'er done!"

I want to see if Keaton and Kate try to have a girl. I want to see who Katie marries and see if she has any kids. I want to watch Josh move his stepkids into college and see Kristin flourish in her career. I want to see Jordan take the hill in whatever final career she settles into and the kind of kind, tall, beautiful woman, my granddaughter, Merak Reneé, will become. I often think of my dad warning me to slow down a little. Since I discovered my work passion late in life, I want to run full-out in a sprint every day! I wanted to be a lobbyist after I was one. I wanted to be a great HR person after I was a mediocre one. I wanted to be a great public speaker after that Bluebird bus talk with the senators. I wanted to play music for hundreds of people, even if for free, and I wanted to give it away for the food bank. And now I am in a race to deliver this book and its companion workbook and then one more. I have plans. And though I feel forty years old, I get reminded frequently enough that I am almost seventy years old. I seemed to be late for most of the significant moves in my life. So I am charging hard to lean into the finish tape.

What are you late for? Not everyone finishes the game. Kyla got pulled from the mound in her sixth inning. I would need extra innings just to do the travel Reneé and I dream about. And I want to light up life's scoreboard with her. I want to be on this world's kiss cam. When I sat at Red Rocks while James and Henry Taylor sang "You Can Close

Your Eyes" as the finale, all I could think about was waiting for Reneé's pathology report. Tears streamed from my face. I'm sure Josh thought I was moved by the song, and I was, but it was about Reneé and not the fact that I want that song played at my funeral. Now I know Reneé and I have another chance to get our list done.

Kyla's passing served as a stark reminder of the unpredictability of life and the reality of mortality. This realization prompted me to take stock of what I have left undone. One of my superficial bucket list items was to own a Mini Cooper like some of the Beatles owned. My heritage is British, and my master's degree is from a UK red brick college, so the Mini made sense—to me!

I am not a patient man. When I head out to "look at cars," Reneé always tells me, "Hey, we aren't buying today, right? We are just looking." It rarely works out that way. I came home that day with a Mini Cooper four-door hardtop, white-pepper-colored with beautiful brown, quilted Chesterfield leather and a panoramic sunroof. It was a dream car! It was half the cost of any vehicle in our now fleet of three cars. I know many of you Corvette and Land Rover people are thinking, *That's not a late-life crisis car, Branch!* I know, and it rides like I'm being dragged in a box across a boulder field and is super expensive to maintain. When I got it, I didn't know about the cult-like owners' clubs, the nine rules, and the rubber duck exchanges, and I was supposed to give it a name. Being of British heritage, I named "her" "Penny Lane." My name is Rodney Lane, and my son is Joshua Lane, so it seemed to follow that Penny Lane should be her name. "Penny Lane" was an old Beatles song, if you hadn't made the connection. A friend, Kaylee, in her twenties, overheard me talking about Penny Lane at a party and about all the things I had bought her and planned for her, and she didn't catch that Penny was a car. She asked, "What in the hell is Rod talking about? Is he in a relationship with someone else? I'm going to have to have a word to protect my little Reneé," whom she calls NayNay! Reneé talks about Penny like she is some sidepiece. I enjoy it, and there is no earthly reason why we need a third car for two people. Funny, my backup plan for financing this book would be to sell Penny Lane and then buy another one later, once I could pay myself back.

The value here is living life to the fullest and not waiting for the "perfect" time to pursue dreams and desires. I encourage you to prioritize experiences and goals that bring you joy and fulfillment, recognizing that life is fragile and time is limited. By acting on your bucket list items, education goals, relationship repairs, etc., you honor your own aspirations and make the most of the present moment.

This concept extends to the people in your life. Telling them how much they mean to you is never a waste of time and energy. Seize the moment as often as you think about it. And you can never start too early. Don't wait until someone is deathly ill to let them know. There is that foundational idea of "caring" again.

Live in the present, and don't wait for the "perfect" time to pursue your dreams and goals. Act and make the most of the opportunities you have. Seize the moment.

Week 47

Love fills life's gaps with kindness.

"What the World Needs Now Is Love"
—Jackie DeShannon

Life Lesson

As a dad to the girls I chose, the ones who came with the deal with Reneé, I learned that a little love and caring goes a long way, especially when their biological dad was absent and they needed the "dad effect" in their lives. I found the same phenomenon occurring in situations outside our family every day. Maslow was right again. People just want to belong, to be seen and heard, to be understood and valued. With the girls, I found myself in multiple situations where some of their girlfriends' dads were absent. The dads were either living far away or were disconnected through relationship and life circumstances. Some of these wonderful, unbridled young souls were just great people whose company we enjoyed. They were always at our house. They were fun and well-adjusted and missing their "dad effect." If we found one at a dance recital whose parents couldn't or didn't attend, Reneé and I made sure they had flowers at the end of the show. We found that it didn't take much to connect with them when love was the motivator. We had no idea about the long-term impact on us or them. They loved us back.

Some of my favorite times were when I chaired the "Daughters and Dads" outing for the high school dance team. I changed the previous name of "Father-Daughter" for the sake of those people who were surrogate fathers, stepdads, or "dads." We would rent a fifty-five-passenger bus and load it with dads and dancers early on a Saturday morning. We would drive to a fun restaurant and entertainment complex on Clear Lake near Houston. I would emcee trivia games from the microphone at the front of the bus. There was laughter for days. At the Boardwalk, the girls would shop, and the dads would buy everything from tickets to carnival rides to belly-button piercing jewelry; the moms were not around, so the dads were unsupervised. There were several girls whose dads couldn't make it or were not in their lives. I made sure the invitation made it very clear that there were plenty of dads to go around. I got to be that "dad effect" to several of these girls for the day. The best part was, I got to be the dad effect for more than just a day for a few of them. It was a dad effect that still warms my heart today—at every chance meeting.

Stephanie (Stephers to us), Jenny ("My Jenny," said in a Forrest Gump voice), Ashley (Ash), and others are still great friends today, more than two decades later. I was in a "chat" with my Jenny last night. I told her how much our relationship meant to Reneé and me, adding so much joy and laughter to our suburban world. And she said some nice things about me and "NayNay" that brought a tear to my eye. She mentioned that ours was a "lifelong friendship" and that is what she valued most. In a recurring theme of this book, if you care just a little and often, the impact somehow is multiplied in the hearts of those receiving your caring gestures.

Hey, and it's a thing. Amit Kumar (University of Texas at Austin) and Nicholas Epley (University of Chicago) in a 2022 study demonstrated what they call the "undervaluing impact" phenomenon. People consistently underestimate how meaningful their expressions of gratitude are to others. We underestimate the emotional impact that an overture of caring or love has on a person.

It is daybreak today; I am staring out the window of our friend Sandi's century-old farmhouse near Lake Placid. I am struck by the fleeting nature of life and its often unwitnessed beauty—like the first rays of morning sun illuminating the church steeple across the river. It's the simple things, like caring, that matter most in a well-lived life. Jenny's chat warmed my heart. Those kids, now adults aged thirty-five to forty, have only a glimpse of what they still mean to Reneé and me. Thank you, Katie and Jordan, for showing me what "dad effect" love can be. Show love as often as you have the opportunity. Fill life's gaps with kindness.

Week 48

Accept that miracles might be evidence that we don't understand it all ... yet.

"Something"
—*The Beatles*

Life Lesson

When my parents lived in Egypt, my twelve-year-old son, Josh, and I went to visit them. They had a lovely home just outside downtown Cairo, with two Bedouin men stationed day and night on the edge of the street. They were "guards" in the loosest sense of the word, though their real job seemed to be watching the world go by.

My dad had a driver named Ahmed, who took them anywhere they needed to go. As part of our two-week visit, we planned a road trip from Cairo across the Gulf of Suez following the Sinai Peninsula to Sharm El Sheikh, then inland to climb Mount Sinai. I carried *The Bible as History* and a topographical map, tracing the Israelites' journey from Egypt.

Along the route, oases appeared at nearly perfect one-day walking intervals—just as the Bible described. One by one, we found them. Whether you take the Bible literally or see it as a collection of representative stories, those details felt faith-building.

We arrived at Mount Sinai and Saint Catherine's Monastery, which has stood, in some form or another, since the sixth century. Two routes led up the mountain: the camel trail, a long, winding gravel path, or a steep staircase straight to the top. We were told the steps were brutal on the knees, so we chose the camel trail. We set out on our "climb."

My mom, who was acrophobic, stayed behind. It was me, Josh, my dad, and Ahmed, the driver. After an hour of steady climbing, Josh suddenly dropped to one knee, clutching his chest. My heart sank. This was a healthy kid. In that moment, two emotions collided: deep concern that my son might be in real medical trouble, miles from any help, and disappointment that we might not make the climb after coming so far.

I knelt beside him and tried to assess the problem. He started feeling a bit better, so I offered to carry him as far as I could to give him some relief. In hindsight, which was pure *Top Gun* energy, my ego was writing checks my body couldn't cash.

Then something remarkable happened. We hadn't seen another soul on the trail all morning. But just as I started to lift Josh, a Bedouin appeared around the bend, walking down the camel trail, leading two camels. Ahmed negotiated a quick deal, and moments later we were swaying our way up the trail atop camels.

At the end of the camel route, we took the steps the rest of the way to the summit. At the top stood a small basilica. The air felt different there—thin, cool, sacred. The camels appearing out of nowhere and the moment of commitment to carry my son were unexplainable. At least the timing was unexplainable.

It reminded me of the Abraham and Isaac story. Different mountains, different eras, but the parallel was clear: The test wasn't about completion; it was about commitment.

As a scientist, I believe there's an explanation for everything—we just don't always have all the data yet. My faith is that one day those connections among events, among people, among even the world's religions will all make sense. Until then, I'm content to call that day on Mount Sinai what it felt like in the moment—a miracle.

Inventory your miracles.

Commit to journaling your wins.

Spend time with the ones you love. Schedule the time. Calendar it.

Be open to tiny miracles. They happen all the time, and they can be easy to miss. The world is more magical when you are open to them. Watch with an open heart, and I can almost assure you that one will happen for you today.

Week 49

Grief seeks truth.

"Tears in Heaven"

—Eric Clapton

Life Lesson

Kim Scott writes about the need for raw truth in her book *Radical Candor*. In the second edition, she doubles down on the idea with one huge caveat: You must have built a relationship with the other person before the truth can be accepted.[44] Grief is an interesting little emotion. How often do you see families reunited with it? How often does it open old wounds?

Sometimes, it takes standing at the edge of loss to realize that life is too short to hide who we really are. I was asked to speak at my Aunt Marie's funeral. Likely, they wanted me because there was no one else to do it. Close family members couldn't keep it together to do it. Those outside the chalk circle didn't have enough context. And the previous funeral services were a disaster because the funeral home officiants simply gave the boilerplate Christian lesson, which was dry, unrelated to the interred, and way too formal for our little family.

In considering what I might say, I recalled having had some great times with this lady, and I needed to make a point about our Christian heritage. I decided I would start with our great grandfather, a Baptist preacher, and follow the scarlet thread through my dad and my aunt down to me. I got a tattoo about fifteen years ago. It is a cross anchor with the cross part highlighted in red. I wanted to end with that belief system flowing through to me using the tattoo. The problem was that my family of origin didn't know and maybe would not approve of the tattoo.

Well, with my Aunt Marie's sense of humor being as sturdy and headstrong as a steel magnolia, it felt like an appropriate ending to the message. There I was, in front of God and everyone, telling them about my religious tattoo from the bunker of the pulpit in the middle of all their grief. That moment was rich with layered life lessons, courage, timing, authenticity, and even the strange clarity that grief can bring. I was honoring her by choosing truth. I took a moment of collective reflection and turned it into a quiet act of liberation. For years, I held a secret out of fear of judgment or rejection. But at that moment, I chose authenticity over approval. The lesson is that you don't owe the world a version of yourself that feels safer and less true. And sometimes the most powerful way to honor someone's memory is to stop hiding the truth.

My mom wasn't upset, at least not to my face, and she congratulated me on a great message. I don't think she had ever heard me speak to a crowd like that, even though it had become a large part of my professional life. I knew my own vulnerability and that my love for our aunt would show through and anchor the message.

Marcus Buckingham, in his book *First, Break All the Rules*, argues that authentic leaders build trust and credibility by being open about their motivations, encouraging genuine feedback, and leading with empathy.[45] The same is true in families and relationships. Bringing your whole self to a relationship creates mutual respect and interdependency. The life lesson here is about how grief often opens a door of authenticity. It brings a connection that was never formed or had been forgotten. When we live authentically, we inspire those around us to do the same, creating a ripple effect of honesty, trust, and deeper relationships. Remember, the courage to be authentic and vulnerable, when built on caring, is the foundation of a fulfilling and meaningful life. Be authentic with kindness.

And you don't have to wait for a family tragedy to start.

Week 50

Give peace a chance.

"Imagine"

—John Lennon

Life Lesson

There is a battle going on among the generations today. What happened? Was I asleep for the past forty years? Workers, and maybe just people, are different today. When I listen to radio news channels, I hear an absurd number of commercials about wiping out your credit card debt, reducing or eliminating your IRS tax bills, or waving some magic wand to get out of that timeshare agreement you knowingly signed. These ads have become the anthem of a group of workers who are looking for an escape hatch. My friend Troy at work calls it the "mulligan mentality." You remember that term from golf, a free do-over when your first shot goes horribly wrong.

Now, at the risk of turning this week's life lesson into a "back in my day" rant about values, hard work, or the meaning of "a good life," let's get one thing straight: In my early career, we could not depend on a bailout for IRS debt, school debt, or credit card debt relief. No one was coming to our rescue. That's not a bias for or against anyone. That's just reality.

We don't understand it, but it is empirically true. The workplace *is* changing, and some of us using our 1980s reference frame can't make sense of it. It's kind of like climate change. You can't argue that summers are hotter, winters are colder, and there are more tropical storms and floods than in the past few decades, but I'm not sure we understand enough about it to blame it on fossil fuels. I mean, the Great Lakes were formed when giant glaciers melted and receded to leave the Great Lakes. What caused the global warming and glacial melting back then? It wasn't fossil fuel! So even though we don't understand the current workforce, we can't deny that it is different.

Anyone believing there will be a bailout every time they fail to deliver on a goal, objective, or bargain has a different view than I did growing up. I'll leave it at that.

We're in an era of radical change. During this disruption, workers are demanding to work from anywhere and with higher wages untethered to skill, output, or economic feasibility. It's as if we're trying to redesign the world of work without acknowledging the scaffolding that's still holding it up.

And here's where it gets tricky: The aged end of the workforce and those watching from the retirement bleachers see this change and are struggling to lead through it. They're holding on to familiar definitions of "accountability." But maybe, just maybe, they're also holding on a little too tightly. As 38 Special sings, "Hold on loosely, but don't let go."[46] I'm not here to say the older folks are right. Lord knows, when Google fails me, I call my kids to ask about the difference among various USB connections, and they ask me what it was like to have coffee with Abraham Lincoln. I'm saying the *language* of leadership has changed, and not everyone has been taught how to speak it. The older citizens grew up in a world where you took the job you could get, worked hard, and earned your stripes. That's what got many of us here. There was no getting a doctor's note submitting that your anxiety prevents you from having in-person meetings. *That is happening.*

I'm not nostalgic about struggling. I'm nostalgic about what struggling teaches us.

The generations that came before and from the beginning of time built many of the processes that we are now automating. That's a win, and someone still needs to understand how we got here.

Here's the uncomfortable truth: Accountability is not a generational trait; it's a human one. And accountability today means more than just showing up on time. It means having a bit of humility, respecting the people who came before, and offering grace to those still learning the new ropes. The world of work is changing. The fundamentals haven't. Character still matters. Ownership still matters. And every generation, regardless of their tools or timelines, has a duty to *step up*. And we must be curious and learn how the other generations learn and how they add value, even if the approach is different.

Working together requires patience. The old guard had no sabbaticals, unlimited paid time off, or an option to work from home. So they will have to give a little. We are going to have to lean in and listen generously to one another, respect each other's truths. Even if you believe in your heart that no one can hold you accountable for a loan or a tax or a timeshare you committed to, know that there are others who believe differently. The workplace has some nonnegotiable requirements. The premise that you must provide more value than the organization expends for your service is still a thing. The workplace is changing, and people are no less valuable just because they think differently. A little caring can go a long way here.

So, maybe, for the world of work today, someone *comes* to your aid some of the time? Accountability may look different than it did forty years ago.

Give peace a chance.

Week 51

Strive to leave behind a unique contribution to this world.

"The Living Years"
—*Mike and The Mechanics*

Life Lesson

My mother was a lover of history. She had a soft spot for biographies of great leaders and lived for the Camelot years of the Kennedy administration. Her favorite reading chair always had a stack of books beside it, dog-eared and underlined, with notes in the margins. During the early '90s, my parents were living in Moscow, where my father was leading an oil field joint venture in the Russian Arctic. Each year, they'd make a long trip back to the US to restock medications and foods they couldn't get overseas.

One year, I had an idea: I was scheduled for a lobbying trip to Washington, DC, and invited my mom to meet me there, her first time visiting the nation's capitol. This was before 9/11, so access to government buildings was more relaxed. I had already arranged a tour of the White House and even secured a seat for her at a Senate breakfast meeting I was attending. When I asked what she wanted to see most, she surprised me: "I want to go to the US Patent Office in Alexandria and see your patent." I had earned a US patent, number 5,083,614, issued on January 28, 1992, for a tool I'd invented as an engineer. To my knowledge, no prototype was ever built, and it was certainly no cure for cancer or groundbreaking algorithm. But it was mine.

We navigated the building's archives and eventually found our way to the old microfiche machines. We slid in the film, adjusted the focus, and there it was: my name, the diagrams, the claims. My mother beamed. To her, it meant that something I'd created might outlive us. And maybe one day my grandson might stumble upon it and say, "That was Papaw's patent."

But my true contribution to humanity came later, though I may be the only person who sees it that way. I had transitioned from engineering and lobbying into human resources. I was leading HR for field teams filled with tough, straight-talking, no-nonsense workers, most of them football fans, most of them skeptical of anything labeled "soft skills." I was trying to get through to them about behavior, about sexual harassment, inclusion, respect, and lecturing didn't work. HR had become the department of don'ts. The "naysayers." Clipboard police. That's when the idea hit me: football. Everyone in the room knew the meaning of a yellow penalty flag.

I started bringing one with me to meetings. If someone cracked a sexist joke, dropped a racial slur, or stitched together a tapestry of expletives, I wouldn't lecture. I'd just throw the flag. Right on the table. Sometimes against the wall. If I heard it through my office door, I'd toss the flag into the hallway. At first, people laughed. "Uh oh." Then they'd ask, "What did I say?" That was the moment I knew I had something. I wasn't just correcting behavior; I was coaching it. In real time. With humor and respect. The flag became a tool of accountability, not judgment. A visible reminder of the standards we aspired to, not the rules we feared.

It spread like wildfire. I started bringing extra flags to every company I joined. I still keep a drawer full in my office. A six-dollar flag became a symbol of culture change, and it helped HR stop being the department of "No" and become the partner that says, "Here's how."

If there's one lesson I've learned, it's this: If you want to make a difference, meet people where they are. Speak their language. Align with their goals. And when you can, leave something behind, something they'll remember. Some people leave patents. Some people leave books. Others just leave a yellow flag, fluttering in memory, reminding someone to do better.

Week 52

Legacy is being someone to someone.

"You'll Be in My Heart"
—Phil Collins

Life Lesson

As I have mentioned earlier, on a Houston train trestle, graffiti reads simply, "Be Someone." To me, it's more than words on steel; it's a reminder to be someone to someone. Legacy begins in those ordinary moments when you help another person believe in themselves. It's affirming to hear someone say, "Sarah Kouba, I just want to have a front row seat to the rest of your life." Or simply, "Thank you, Hang Bower [pronounced "Hong"], for being so thoughtful." Legacy is created in those small affirmations that stay with people long after the words are spoken.

Legacy doesn't need grand gestures. It often shows up in unplanned kindness like buying Girl Scout cookies just to give them back so someone else can enjoy them, playing music for free because you love how it brings people together, or supporting a friend's seemingly hairbrained scheme before you fully understand it, only to discover later they were on to something big. Each of these moments plants a seed that may grow in ways you never expected.

For me, legacy lives most tangibly around my own table. My wife, Reneé, our sons, daughters, grandchildren, and chosen family carry the story of who we are. Our life together is rich with connection, grounded in love, and full of lessons learned the slow, hard way. Legacy doesn't live in things, though things may remind us of amazing people or events. Legacy lives in stories retold, in the values passed down through generations, and in the belonging we've built together.

It also extends into the workplace. Two HR managers from my past teams went on to earn the top HR jobs at large companies. That validates legacy in its own way—our legacy together. Hopefully, at least one principle or practice we shared together shaped the leader they've become. Legacy at work isn't measured in job titles but in the ripple effect of values, practices, and courage instilled in others.

Maslow reminded us that the most meaningful parts of life are rooted in connection, attention, and belonging. I experienced this vividly at the wedding of our friends Doug and Rudy in Mexico. At that time, I was still processing my feelings about same-sex marriage. Reneé and I chose to sponsor the welcome toast. We brought etched tequila glasses with two little grooms, arranged wildflowers in empty tequila boxes, and filled copper pans with ice. The toast was simple: "Thank you for opening our hearts. Thank you for giving us perspective. Thank you for letting us feel something deeper than expected." That night, they left a legacy with us. Legacy is often born in those unexpected intersections of love, perspective, and courage.

Legacy isn't your name on a building, a plaque, an Instagram bio, or the amount of money left behind. Legacy isn't about volume or visibility, it's about depth. It is how people feel about you when you are no longer present and how they carry that feeling forward. Legacy is the result of a life well-lived, instilled with integrity over time. It is built in quiet rooms, in conversations, with listening ears and little acts of kindness that make others feel significant, seen, and valued.

The whole point of the book *Who Not How*, by Dan Sullivan with Benjamin Hardy, is that legacy doesn't live in what you created or how you created it. That's just the bookmark. Legacy lives in who you helped and who helped you. It lives in front porch coffees, long walks, and deep conversations. It grows through listening, the kind of listening that invites someone to lean in, to trust, and to feel valued.

Legacy is not loud, but it echoes. It is not flashy, but it lasts. It is not forced, but it is remembered. What's one quiet moment you didn't think mattered at the time but later realized helped shape someone's path? What are you doing today that will echo long after your name fades from the thank-you card?

Live the kind of life worth retelling. Because as Dr. Seuss reminds us,

> *"To the world you may be one person.*
> *But to one person, you may be the world."*

The End

Afterword

By Gair Maxwell

Author of *Big Little Legends, How Everyday Leaders Build Irresistible Brands*
Speaker of the Year by TEC Canada, Brand Strategist, Tennessee Squire
7-Time Runner Up on the M.G.A. Golf Tour

Did you skip right to the end to read the afterword?

Maybe you did ... maybe you didn't because in many respects the book you are holding in your hands represents anyone's life journey. You decide where you want to start. Where you want to finish. How you want to get there.

Since we're here at the end, I thought you may want the inside scoop on a few things about the author most people wouldn't know. In fact, you could have titled this afterword as "*This Is The Rod I Know*".

It was March of 2025 when Rod Branch wandered into an executive boardroom at a Houston-area golf club and sat in on my signature presentation for local members of a CEO Peer Advisory network known as Vistage Worldwide. And it was through the course of a program known as BIG LITTLE LEGENDS, that Rod separated himself from the rest of the group by leaning in.

Listening with genuine curiosity.

Writing notes.

Fully attentive and asking questions.

In other words, Rod was one of the rare few in that room that day who was eager to better understand the depth of the material and how it could be applied in real world situations.

And that's when the magic happened.

Towards the end of the program, Rod stood and shared the story about a golfing trip that he and his father had taken to St. Andrews, Scotland. In a very personal, heartfelt way, Rod spoke about how much that one round of golf had meant to his Dad and why the photograph of his father and him posing on the iconic Swilcan Bridge is the centrepiece of a Houston man cave known as the 'Bourbon Room'.

Being the only son of a former professional golfer who was born minutes from the first tee at the Old Course in St. Andrews and as a lover of all things Jack Daniels, it was only natural that Rod and I bonded right away. Like so many of the chapters in this book, it's like the universe already had a plan for us. We just stepped in and went along for the ride.

That's the Rod I know and that's what makes this book and the many kernels of wisdom discovered within so valuable.

He is a real student of this great game called life. Always looking for ways to shave a few strokes off his scorecard while helping others do the same.

As a reader, you would want to know that this book was not something generated by trendy digital shortcuts designed to wipe the humanity away from what is supposed to be a very personal experience between you and the author. You would like to know that the man who put his name on the cover actually did the back-breaking work demanded of any credible author. A whiskey-drinking, guitar-playing truth seeker who wrote from a place of being sincerely curious about the significant events that shaped his life, what there was to learn, and how to spread those insights across 52 weeks of an entire calendar year.

In a world more fleeting and fake ... I often wonder if there are still people who ache... for that which is permanent and real? If so, that's what *Week Minded* represents. A real-life, warts-and-all account of his journey and the lessons learned along the way.

"The Rod I Know" is the same one who shows up in these pages; a fellow traveller, thirsting for every last drop of this drink called life; an author who created this 52-week guide to help anyone of us find our way home.

About the People Who Shaped This Book

This book isn't fiction. The people in it? Very real. Quirky, brilliant, stubborn, funny, flawed, wise, just like your people. They are my family, my friends, my mentors, and my memory-keepers. Some share my bloodline, others married in, some just wandered into my life and never left. All of them helped write this book, whether they meant to or not.

Let's start with the woman who's had a front row seat to this dumpster-fire chaos since 1994: **Reneé Lorainne Branch**, RN, my wife, my TV series junkie partner, my late-night therapist, and the reason I didn't stay "riddled with self-doubt," to steal a line from James Taylor's brother, Livingston Taylor's song, "Going Round One More time." She's the one who nudged me back to college in my fifties and cheered as I climbed that mountain.

Thank you, **Dr. Taryn Marie**, best-selling author of *The Five Practices of Highly Resilient People*, for inspiring me to be vulnerable and to tell my story that led to my own staying power so that others would be brave enough to tell theirs. And thank you for your advice and for moving forward with my foreword. "See what I did there!" It's our inside joke.

Thank you, **Gair Maxwell**, best-selling author of *Big Little Legends*, for helping me see my value. Thank you for agreeing to write the afterword for this book, and I really value our shared legacy of the Old Course at St. Andrews, our dads, and being fellow Tennessee Squires.

Then there are my sons, **Keaton** and **Josh**, who have grown into men I admire and whose lives are anything but boring. Add in my chosen daughters, **Katie** and **Jordan**, and my daughters-in-law, **Kristin** and **Dr. Kate**, and what you get is a family potluck of intelligence, wit, strength, and soul. At the time of this writing, **Merak** and **Ashton** are the OG grandkids and the unofficial sunshine in every room. **Walker** and **Laia**, curious and smart, who joined the crew as bonus grandkids through Kristin, are already stealing hearts. Josh, now a stepdad, is proving that his arms are plenty wide enough to hold their hopes and dreams.

My parents, **Lynden "Dawn"** and **Billy Ray Branch**, taught me the value of hard work, hard laughs, and hard times. My dad liked to say, "We didn't start with nothing; it took us a while to get up to nothing." That tells you everything about our family's blend of humility and humor.

My sisters, **Anna** and **Becky**, shared my childhood and somehow still speak to me, despite my storytelling liberties. If that's not the way it was then, that's the way it was now. Anna fights cancer with science in Oklahoma, and Becky fights ignorance with chalkboards in Wyoming. Both are smarter than me. I've made peace with that.

Our **grandparents**, the Branches and the Foremans, were living proof that roots matter. On one side: dirt-under-the-fingernails, sharecropping grit. On the other: a grandfather missing fingers on one hand who could twirl a screwdriver with the best of them and his father who floated timber down Louisiana's Calcasieu River and supplemented his income as a bare-knuckle brawler. It's no wonder I'm a storyteller.

Thank you to **Julian Franklin Pugh** who not only has become a great friend but has given me great advice as a published author himself. Thank you for the early morning coaching sessions and copious amounts of coffee.

Thank you to **Sue Burnett**, **Dr. Juliet Breeze**, **Janette Marx**, **Hang Bower, Heidi Peters**, **Sarah Kouba**, **Madison Townsend**, **Liz Townsend**, and **Alan Brush** for bravely, and with the kindest critiques, letting me know how the book made you feel and where it could take other readers.

On LinkedIn in 2025, where many of these stories first appeared, **Lynette LeBlanc** and **Leah Kasparek** both encouraged me to consider writing a book containing these anecdotes and stories. Thank you to each of you for your friendship and for your heart.

As for my chosen family, oh, the characters! **Liz Townsend** and **Jared Hamilton** are my kindred spirits, well beyond leadership mind melds and more than being a second and third brain—yes, we operate that way. Here's to many years of co-presenting and co-creating content. **Wendell Schuman** reminds me that "it all adds up." **Darryl Preen** swears "better is better." **Jonathan Risch**, a boss for a handful of years and friend for nearly thirty years, taught me that real leadership doesn't need a spotlight. **Mary Ellen Coombe**, who bent my career toward HR at a time I needed it. **Hang** and **Corey Bower**, **Aaron Sobel**, **Christine Brinkley**, **Stacey Brown**, **Kellee Webb**, **Denise Espinoza**, **Suzanne Speak**, **Bob Newhouse**, **Barbara Lane**, **Jennifer Lane**, **Chuck Heaton**, **Chuck Niederhofer**, **Chuck Kemper**, and others too many to mention, my HR deep thinkers, were always encouraging. **Lijo**, **Laura**, **Emily**, **Amanda**, **Kholo**, **Dan, Janean**, **Jackie**, who are my next-level HR "lean-ons."

Thank you, **Tommy John**, for getting me healthy again and for the early coffee talks, and **Adam**, **Ryan**, **Maggie**, **Monica**. **Heather**, **Tom**, **Tracy**, **Patty** and **Kevin,** my friends in (not with) benefits. Sol Perez, your friendship is fierce and faithful. You are a good man. **Larry** and **Linda Gibbs**, you've been my music family for decades. And Larry, your honest critique of my live performances? That's a rare gift. I trust your ears more than my own.

Thank you to the family of **Dick Lynn** (**Karen**, **Allison**, and **Brian**) for sharing your partner/dad with me. I miss him every day. And thank you to my extended family of friends inside the chalk circle, the **Burckles**, **Wakefords**, **Myers**, **Hortons**, and **Raymors**—may we age gracefully.

Now, if you haven't seen your name here, don't worry. There's a solid chance you appear somewhere in these fifty-two lessons, maybe disguised as "a friend," "a mentor," or "the guy with the great advice I never asked for and desperately needed." The list of people who shaped me is too long for these pages.

About the Author

Rod Branch, musician, engineer, lobbyist, executive, inventor, ordained minister, and now, author. He is a grassroots American having worked as a roustabout in the oil fields of small-town America and on to engineer in the Alaskan Arctic, Washington lobbyist, and C-suite officer. His career has seen many industries, including energy, manufacturing, and construction. Rod holds a bachelor of science degree in petroleum engineering technology from Oklahoma State University and a master of science degree in global human resource management from the University of Liverpool (UK). He studied industrial relations at Cornell and has spoken at national leadership, safety, and management conferences nationwide. He is a frequent guest lecturer at Texas A&M University, holds US patent number 5083614, and is both an ordained minister and a professional musician. He received the *Houston Business Journal*'s HR Impact Leader of the Year award in 2024 and was honored to be named a Tennessee Squire and an honorary admiral in the Texas Navy in 2025 for his various charity efforts during COVID. He is a husband, father, grandfather, dog guy, and bourbon enthusiast. He is inspired holding his grandchildren, watching it snow in Breckenridge, Colorado, or sipping coffee while deer wander across the Barton Creek Resort in Austin, Texas. His hope is that this book inspires you to keep learning, leading, and living with purpose and to find meaning in the ordinary moments that build enduring confidence—one week, one story, one act of kindness at a time.

The Story of BranchWater Press

As with many stories in my life, this one begins with music. As a self-taught guitarist with physical limitations of small hands and fingers that don't bend like other people's, it took a long time to get good enough to allow others to hear me. I finally emerged from the back of the house, brave enough to begin playing guitar and singing in front of people. My younger son, Keaton, was already an accomplished guitarist and singer. He graciously allowed me to play with him, and he would fill in with harmonies and lead guitar licks. He made me sound better than I was. We were overheard playing around the house, and a friend asked if we would play for a kid's birthday party for free. We agreed and played for about an hour or so at a party in a park. A few days later, we got a call asking how much we charged for gigs, and they booked us to open a hair salon. Yes, a hair salon grand opening. The gig took off and we needed a name, so we came up with BranchWater. The logo was a tree. Being a bourbon enthusiast, branch often refers to branch water, as in fresh from a stream, as a mixer with bourbon and is referred to as "bourbon and branch." BranchWater seemed perfect.

Eventually, Keaton went to work for Apple in retail, and he never knew his work schedule from week to week, so we had to stop gigging. As I was sadly packing the BranchWater banner away in the garage, Keaton looked at me and said, "Dad, you can do this as a solo musician." I told him I didn't think I was good enough for that, but he begged to differ. I did go on to a solo career for twenty years, but I played under Rod Branch Music. The name BranchWater still spawned fond memories of gigging with my son and the connection to bourbon and branch.

So when the opportunity arose to name the LLC and the publishing company, BranchWater seemed to be the way to go. From the music roots of my dad's cornet that changed our lives to my son's and my professional music careers, BranchWater and BranchWater Press live on, continuing the musical theme of our lives.

Notes

[1]Taryn Marie Stejskal, *The 5 Practices of Highly Resilient People*, (New York: Hachette Books, 2023), x.

[2]Marcus Buckingham, *Love + Work: How to Find What You Love, Love What You Do, and Do It for the Rest of Your Life* (Boston: Harvard Business Review Press, 2022), 63.

[3]Marcus Buckingham, *Love + Work: How to Find What You Love, Love What You Do, and Do It for the Rest of Your Life*, 69.

[4]Julia Cameron, *The Artist's Way: A Spiritual Path to Higher Creativity* (New York: G. P. Putnam's Sons, 1992), 9–15.

[5]Anne Lamott, *Bird by Bird: Some Instructions on Writing and Life* (New York: Anchor Books, 1995), 21–22.

[6]Stephen M. R. Covey, *The Speed of Trust: The One Thing That Changes* Everything, narrated by the author (Free Press, 2006), at 45:34 of "Core 2 Intent."

[7]Don Miguel Ruiz, *The Four Agreements: A Practical Guide to Personal Freedom* (San Rafael, CA: Amber-Allen Publishing, 1997), 48.

[8]Taryn Marie Stejskal, *The 5 Practices of Highly Resilient People*, narrated by the author (New York: Hachette Books, Audible, 2023).

[9]Abraham H. Maslow, *Motivation and Personality*, 3rd ed. (New York: Harper & Row, 1987).

[10]John C. Maxwell, *The 21 Irrefutable Laws of Leadership* (Nashville: Thomas Nelson, 1998), 47.

[11]Jim Collins, *Good to Great: Why Some Companies Make the Leap . . . and Others Don't* (New York: Harper Business, 2001), 121.

[12]Simon Sinek, *Start with Why: How Great Leaders Inspire Everyone to Take Action* (New York: Portfolio, 2009), 1.

[13]Heather R. Younger, *The Art of Caring Leadership: How Leading with Heart Uplifts Teams and Organizations* (Oakland, CA: Berrett-Koehler, 2021).

[14]Marcus Buckingham, *Love + Work: How to Find What You Love, Love What You Do, and Do It for the Rest of Your Life*, 63.

[15]Taryn Marie Stejskal, *The 5 Practices of Highly Resilient People*, x.

[16]Zig Ziglar, *See You at the Top* (Gretna, LA: Pelican Publishing, 1975), 32.

[17]Becca Levy, *Breaking the Age Code: How Your Beliefs About Aging Determine How Long and Well You Live*, narrated by the author (New York: Harper Audio, 2022), at 40:11 of chap. 6.

[18]Jess Ekstrom, *Chasing the Bright Side: Embrace Optimism, Activate Your Purpose, and Write Your Own Story*, narrated by the author (New York: Penguin Audio, 2019), at 27:47 of chap. 2.

[19]Rhonda Byrne, *The Secret*, (New York: Simon & Schuster, 2006), 1.

[20]Simon Sinek, host, "The Future You Avoid Is Riskier Than the One You Face," *A Bit of Optimism*, The Optimism Company, podcast, January 15, 2021, Spotify, https://open.spotify.com/episode/063zSo9x4tdpwf3jjfG0lF?si=dodVHFoPRbS4jV6dhSUNUA&nd= 1&dlsi=b8fb022a7fd44bdd.

[21]Adam Grant, "Susan David on Emotional Agility," *WorkLife with Adam Grant*, podcast, TED in partnership with Transmitter Media (formerly Pineapple Street Media) as part of the TED Audio Collective, January 23, 2021.

[22]John C. Maxwell, *The 5 Levels of Leadership: Proven Steps to Maximize Your Potential*, narrated by the author (New York: Center Street Audio, 2011), at 1:50 of "Level 1: Position: It's a Great Place to Visit, but You Wouldn't Want to Live There."

[23]Marcus Buckingham, *Love + Work: How to Find What You Love, Love What You Do, and Do It for the Rest of Your Life*, 147.

[24]Michael Bungay Stanier, *The Coaching Habit: Say Less, Ask More, and Change the Way You Lead Forever* (Toronto, ON, Canada: Box of Crayons Press, 2016), 45.

[25]Brené Brown, *Dare to Lead: Brave Work, Tough Conversations, Whole Hearts*, narrated by the author (New York: Random House, 2018), at 01:27:57 of "Section Three: The Armory."

[26]Zig Ziglar, *See You at the Top*, 36.

[27]Stephen R. Covey, *The Seven Habits of Highly Effective People: Restoring the Character Ethic* (New York: Simon and Schuster 1989), 59.

[28]Mel Robbins, *The Let Them Theory: A Life-Changing Tool That Millions of People Can't Stop Talking About* (Carlsbad, CA: Hay House, 2024), 18.

[29]Stephen M. R. Covey, *The Speed of Trust: The One Thing That Changes Everything* (New York: Simon & Schuster Audio, 2006), 59.

[30]Brené Brown, *Dare to Lead: Brave Work, Tough Conversations, Whole Hearts*, 23–28.

[31]Simon Sinek, *Leaders Eat Last: Why Some Teams Pull Together and Others Don't* (New York: Portfolio/Penguin, 2014), 19.

[32]James Taylor, "Walking Man," Warner Brothers, produced by David Spinozza, June 30, 1975.

[33]Stephen R. Covey, *The 7 Habits of Highly Effective People: Powerful Lessons in Personal Change*, narrated by the author (New York: Simon & Schuster Audio, 1989) at 01:21:29 of "Principles of Personal Management."

[34]Ryan Holiday, *Ego Is the Enemy*, (New York: Portfolio/Penguin, 2016), 16.

[35]Malcolm Gladwell, *Blink: The Power of Thinking Without Thinking*, narrated by the author (New York: Hachette Audio, 2005), chap. 1.

[36]Daniel Kahneman, *Thinking, Fast and Slow*, narrated by Patrick Egan (New York: Farrar, Straus and Giroux Audio, 2011), "Part 1: Two Systems" (chapters 1–9).

[37]Michael R. LeGault, *Think!: Why Crucial Decisions Can't Be Made in the Blink of an Eye*, narrated by Tom Perkins (New York: Simon & Schuster Audio, 2006).

[38]Somer Scandridge (@somerscandridge), "Sometimes I feel like I'm juggling fire while riding a unicycle," Facebook post, June 13, 2025, https://www.facebook.com/share/p/1DBvQXtAuf/.

[39]Sheryl Crow, "No One Said It Would Be Easy," Tuesday Night Music Club (A&M Records, 1993); Coldplay, "The Scientist," on A Rush of Blood to the Head (Parlophone/Capitol Records, 2002).

[40]"American Pie," by Don McLean, produced by United Artists Records, 1971.

[41]"Big Yellow Taxi," by Joni Mitchell, produced by Reprise Records, 1970.

[42]"Believe," by Elton John, produced by Rocket Records, 1995.

[43]Amit Kumar and Nicholas Epley, "Undervaluing Gratitude: Expressers Misunderstand the Consequences of Showing Appreciation," *Journal of Personality and Social Psychology* 119, no. 3 (2020): 587-610.

[44]Kim Scott, *Radical Candor: Be a Kick-Ass Boss Without Losing Your Humanity*, 2nd ed., narrated by the author (New York: Macmillan Audio, 2021).

[45]Marcus Buckingham, *First, Break All the Rules: What the World's Greatest Managers Do Differently*, narrated by Eric Conger (New York: Simon & Schuster Audio, 1999), at 10:56 of chap. 2.

[46]"Hold On Loosely," by 38 Special, produced by A&M Records, 1981.

[47]Dan Sullivan and Benjamin Hardy, *Who Not How: The Formula to Achieve Bigger Goals Through Accelerating Teamwork*, narrated by Dan Sullivan and Benjamin Hardy (New York: Hay House Audio, 2020).

www.ingramcontent.com/pod-product-compliance
Ingram Content Group UK Ltd.
Pitfield, Milton Keynes, MK11 3LW, UK
UKHW060126010826
14089UKWH00020B/261/J

9 798994 293225